T0342526

NINA BOEGER

RETHINKING GOVERNANCE IN PUBLIC SERVICE OUTSOURCING

Private Delivery in Sustainable Ownership

BRISTOL
UNIVERSITY
PRESS

First published in Great Britain in 2024 by

Bristol University Press
University of Bristol
1–9 Old Park Hill
Bristol
BS2 8BB
UK
t: +44 (0)117 374 6645
e: bup-info@bristol.ac.uk

Details of international sales and distribution partners are available at
bristoluniversitypress.co.uk

British Library Cataloguing in Publication Data
A catalogue record for this book is available from the British Library

ISBN 978-1-5292-1284-6 hardcover
ISBN 978-1-5292-1286-0 ePub
ISBN 978-1-5292-1287-7 ePdf

Cover design: Blu Inc
Front cover image: iStock/mbbirdy
Bristol University Press uses environmentally responsible
print partners.
Printed and bound in Great Britain by CPI Group (UK) Ltd,
Croydon, CR0 4YY

Contents

Acknowledgements

My grateful thanks, for supporting this book project in various ways, to Albert Sanchez-Graells, Tony Prosser, David Hunter, Andrew Dean, Tonia Novitz, Charlotte Villiers, Donna Tully and Erik Jamieson. And, above all, to Joe, Lucy and Kiara.

Introduction

A new UK public procurement law

In 2023, the UK Parliament agreed on new public procurement legislation, moving beyond the previous public procurement regime based on European Union (EU) law.[1] Public procurement legislation imposes on the public sector, and bodies with designated public responsibility, obligations to observe structured tender procedures when they contract out public services, especially those above a certain value threshold. It also provides remedies for aggrieved providers that lose out as a consequence of illegal contract awards. These public procurement rules have a variety of objectives, but mostly their aim is to ensure open and transparent tender procedures to maximize the benefit of market competition for the state when it buys goods or services from private suppliers. Where procedures lack transparency or are otherwise uncompetitive, this may restrict the state's choices and lead to suboptimal provider selection, meaning the public sector may not secure value for money, and therefore maximize public benefit, in its procurement.[2]

The new UK public procurement law is one of the first major pieces of legislation to make use of greater freedom following Brexit, with the UK no longer being bound by EU law. The government presented the law as a chance mainly to simplify public procurement, to improve transparency and reduce bureaucracy, to adapt the regime to the UK's current

---

[1] The Procurement Act 2023, hereafter PA2023. The new legislation is expected to come into force in October 2024.

[2] See the procurement objectives set out in section 12(1) PA2023.

procurement needs and to secure better access, especially for small and local providers, to public markets. The law repeals the existing regulations based on EU law and in their stead sets out new rules and procedures for public contracting authorities (including central government departments, their arm's-length bodies and the wider public sector) in the selection of providers for the award of public contracts with a value above the relevant thresholds. It also includes provisions for contracts that fall below those thresholds.

Public procurement law is a complex and technical area of regulation, hardly a popular talking point. Yet in the debates over this new legislation, strong political sentiments and a profound unease with the way in which public contracting has developed in the UK in recent years, in ways that undermine attempts at delivering public value, quickly became apparent. UK government spending on public procurement has risen sharply in recent decades, and it currently accounts for roughly one third of all public spending in the UK. This rising trend is also reflected across Europe and many other developed economies. Decisions over how those monies are spent are critical for the UK's economic trajectory and its attempt to reposition the British economy post Brexit in global trade.[3]

Yet there are now widely evidenced problems in the supply of public contracts, with recurring news of major failures in recent years, particularly in the delivery of more complex public service contracts. Britain was a pioneer in privatizing public services and in outsourcing (contracting to private

---

[3] See the Labour deputy leader's comment in the recent parliamentary debate over the new public procurement legislation: 'When most people hear the word "procurement", they switch off, but I cannot get enough of it. It is absolutely critical to our economy and to our future national prosperity' – Procurement Bill [HL], Angela Rayner Excerpts, 2nd reading, 9 January 2023 [online], Available from: www.parallelpar liament.co.uk/mp/angela-rayner/debate/2023-01-09/commons/comm ons-chamber/procurement-bill-lords [Accessed 23 February 2024].

providers) their delivery back in the 1980s, but since then it has struggled with problems in this field. The UK's Institute for Government, for example, has identified, in the British history of public service outsourcing,

> several factors that consistently resulted in contracts going wrong or failing to meet their objectives. These included low competition, an inability to adequately measure performance, inappropriate risk transfer and poor contract management ... in pursuit of unrealistic cost savings and without a reasonable expectation that companies could deliver efficiencies, innovations or service improvements.[4]

It also found that '[a]cross all services, many of the savings have been achieved by reducing the pay and conditions of staff.'[5] Data for 2023 gave rise to concerns about major private contractors too often missing targets and not performing well against key performance indicators (KPIs).[6]

---

[4] Sasse, T., Nickson, S., Britchfield, C. and Davies, N. (2020) *Government Outsourcing: When and How to Bring Public Services Back into Government Hands* [online], Institute for Government, June, p 11, Available from: www.instituteforgovernment.org.uk/sites/default/files/publicati ons/government-outsourcing-public-services-government-hands.pdf [Accessed 23 February 2024].

[5] Sasse, T., Nickson, S., Britchfield, C. and Davies, N. (2020) *Government Outsourcing: When and How to Bring Public Services Back into Government Hands* [online], Institute for Government, June, p 11, Available from: www.instituteforgovernment.org.uk/sites/default/files/publicati ons/government-outsourcing-public-services-government-hands.pdf [Accessed 23 February 2024].

[6] Cabinet Office (2024) 'Key Performance Indicators (KPIs) for government's most important contracts', *Gov.uk* [online], 25 January, Available from: www.gov.uk/government/publications/key-perf ormance-indicators-kpis-for-governments-most-important-contracts [Accessed 23 February 2024], discussed in Alegretti, A. (2023) 'Rise in outsourced UK government services failing to meet standards', *The*

In the recent past, multiple governance failures in the delivery of key public service contracts, in some cases involving the demise of key corporate providers, have increased pressure on government to implement strategic reform. The advent of COVID-19 only intensified these pressures, giving rise to charges that during the pandemic the UK government awarded additional public contracts with little accountability, including to private firms without a track record in the delivery of healthcare equipment or healthcare services. Delivery failures, including the provision of defective healthcare equipment, eventually left the government out of pocket by billions of pounds. Litigation retrospectively exposed a lack of accountability.[7] A government review into the matter concluded that 'processes and practice' required improvement, including changes to (a) procurement law and policy for contracting in a time of crisis, (b) the government's own process and governance with relation to this law and (c) management of actual or perceived conflicts of interest in a procurement context.[8] At the same time, the COVID-19 'test and trace' system, contracted to large private consultancies, was publicly declared a failure despite 'eye watering' costs.[9]

Guardian [online], 4 August, Available from: www.theguardian.com/business/2023/aug/04/rise-in-outsourced-uk-government-services-failing-to-meet-standards [Accessed 23 February 2024].

[7] Crerar, P. (2023) 'Ministers' procurement bill a "charter for cronies", says Labour', *The Guardian* [online], 9 January, Available from: www.theguardian.com/uk-news/2023/jan/09/ministers-procurement-bill-a-charter-for-cronies-says-labour [Accessed 23 February 2024].

[8] HM Government (2020) *Boardman Review of Government Procurement in the COVID-19 Pandemic* [online], 9 December, p 1, Available from: https://assets.publishing.service.gov.uk/media/60896ff0e90e076ab07a6d83/Boardman_Review_of_Government_COVID-19_Procurement_final_report.pdf [Accessed 23 February 2024].

[9] House of Commons Committee of Public Accounts (2021) *Test and Trace Update: Twenty-Third Report of Session 2021–22* [online], 27 October, pp 3 and 5, Available from: https://committees.parliament.uk/publications/7651/documents/79945/default/ [Accessed 23 February 2024].

The new legislation addresses these issues only partially, although it does improve important aspects of public procurement. Describing the previous EU-based regime as 'bureaucratic and process-driven',[10] the UK legislation introduces new and simplified rules on the selection of providers based on the public procurement objectives of delivering value for money and maximizing public benefit, and the principles of transparency, integrity, non-discrimination and fair treatment.[11] It also requires contracting authorities to take account of broader national strategic priorities which the government will set out periodically in a national procurement policy statement.[12] The first such statement, published in 2021 prior to the enactment of the new legislation, includes as national priority outcomes the creation of new businesses, new jobs and new skills, tackling climate change and reducing waste, and improving supplier diversity, innovation and resilience.[13] Reflecting Brexit, the legislation provides for the UK to meet its international obligations on public procurement, including in the World Trade Organization's Agreement on Government Procurement and the UK's Trade and Cooperation Agreement with the EU. It relies on a string of delegated powers to create secondary legislation filling out further details under the legislation, including for setting the range of those public services that fall under the 'light

---

[10] Cabinet Office (2022) 'Simpler, more flexible and transparent procurement', *Gov.uk* [online], 12 May, Available from: www.gov.uk/government/news/simpler-more-flexible-and-transparent-procurement [Accessed 23 February 2024].

[11] Section 12 PA2023.

[12] Section 13 PA2023.

[13] HM Government (2021) *National Procurement Policy Statement* [online], June, Available from: https://assets.publishing.service.gov.uk/government/uploads/system/uploads/attachment_data/file/990289/National_Procurement_Policy_Statement.pdf [Accessed 23 February 2024].

touch' regime, which allows authorities greater flexibility in awarding contracts.[14]

The law imposes a number of further changes from the previous EU-based regime. These include several measures to make public procurement more accessible for small and medium-sized enterprises (SMEs) and for social providers, which also typically are smaller and locally based organizations, to ensure lower barriers to market entry. The introduction of a new central digital platform for providers, to simplify their registration process and access to bid details, is likely to benefit smaller providers. The new law also strengthens provisions on prompt payment by requiring contracting authorities to pay suppliers within 30 days and to issue payments compliance notices, obligations which also extend to primary contractors in paying their subcontractors.[15] Among other things, it also imposes a duty on contracting authorities to consider whether the goods or services in question could reasonably be supplied under more than one contract, with contracts split into lots.[16] In essence, the government is trying to make it simpler, cheaper and quicker to bid, and aiming to provide for timely payment and further support, including more market engagement, information and opportunities for feedback. It also imposes

---

[14] Section 9 PA2023. See also the draft Procurement Act 2023 (Miscellaneous Provisions) Regulations 2024 [online], Available from: https://assets.pub lishing.service.gov.uk/government/uploads/system/uploads/attachme nt_data/file/1163167/230615_DRAFT_Procurement_Act_2023__ Miscellaneous_Provisions__Regulations_2024_-_consultation_version. pdf [Accessed 23 February 2024].

[15] Sections 68, 69 and 73 PA2023. According to the Labour deputy leader, however, the government 'talks about the trickle-down effect of 30 days, but I do not believe that will work in this instance' – Procurement Bill [HL], Angela Rayner Excerpts, 2nd reading, 9 January 2023 [online], Available from: www.parallelparliament.co.uk/mp/angela-rayner/deb ate/2023-01-09/commons/commons-chamber/procurement-bill-lords [Accessed 27 February 2024].

[16] Section 18 PA2023, replacing the previous regime set out in regulation 46 of the Public Contract Regulations 2015.

on contracting authorities a general duty to have regard to any procurement barriers faced by SMEs. An existing online service to help smaller providers resolve problems in accessing public procurement opportunities continues to operate under the new regime.[17]

Some will regard aspects of this legislation as bold, while others will see aspects as disappointingly incremental, not addressing some key questions. All would likely agree, however, that the legislation itself is only a starting point and that its effectiveness will depend on the extent to which the state manages to implement it effectively, even if it means putting in place additional governance instruments, including regulations, contracting guidance and skills training and monitoring, all of which will require some additional resources. From a political perspective, the parliamentary debate itself offered a revealing commentary on the variety of perspectives on highly contentious issues of public service outsourcing in Britain at the moment. Clearly emerging in some, perhaps surprisingly heated, parliamentary exchanges was concern, expressed mainly by members of the opposition, about the role of corporate actors, driven by shareholder value and often domiciled outside of the UK, 'taking this country for a ride' in gaining access to the most lucrative public service contracts.[18]

Debates in the House of Lords, for example, brought up instances of large corporate providers being awarded lucrative

---

[17] HM Government (2022) 'Public Procurement Review Service progress report 2021-22 (HTML)', *Gov.uk* [online], updated 15 December 2022, Available from: www.gov.uk/government/publications/mystery-shop per-progress-reports/public-procurement-review-service-progress-rep ort-2021-22-html [Accessed 23 February 2024].

[18] Procurement Bill [HL], volume 824, debated on Monday 24 October 2022, Lord Hunt of Kings Heath, column 293GC, Available from https://hansard.parliament.uk/lords/2022-10-24/debates/87250434- 8ABA-40F5-89C3-C1A3E4D5B5F7/ProcurementBill(HL)#contr ibution-8E86E492-3B33-4EE6-95AE-05EF42F51003 [Accessed 23 February 2024].

public contracts repeatedly despite considerable failings in their service provision. On one occasion, describing the government as 'supine in many respects when dealing with these multinational companies', a Lords Member recounted the 'remarkable decision to award Fujitsu a £48 million contract to upgrade the police national computer, given the role of that company in developing Horizon software for the Post Office [faults in which caused one of the largest public outsourcing scandals]'. The account continues:

> We were told by a Minister that in effect, there was no alternative because of the continuing arrangements with that company. Listening to the comments made … about performance issues, corruption, competition infringements, which were added to by my noble friend, and the issues on tax, essentially the Minister has an ideological objection to the use of contracts to further government policy outside the narrow procurement interest. This is where I fundamentally disagree with her.[19]

Another concern focused on the growing 'financialisation and hedge fund or overseas ownership' of provision, including in the most complex person–centred public service sectors, effectively turning highly personalized areas of welfare in our society into profits for shareholder value.[20] One parliamentarian highlighted that 'private companies, including

---

[19] Procurement Bill [HL], volume 824, debated on Monday 24 October 2022, Lord Hunt of Kings Heath, column 293GC, Available from https://hansard.parliament.uk/lords/2022-10-24/debates/87250434-8ABA-40F5-89C3-C1A3E4D5B5F7/ProcurementBill(HL)#contribution-8E86E492-3B33-4EE6-95AE-05EF42F51003 [Accessed 23 February 2024].

[20] Procurement Bill [HL], volume 823, debated on Monday 11 July 2022, Baroness Bennet of Manor Castle, column 342GC, Available

offshore-based private equity companies, have made excessive profits out of care home provision in a number of cases', namechecking 'Terra Firma, which the Minister will recall is based in the Channel Islands'.[21] Another queried low-tax arrangements involving corporate providers of public services, noting that the Bill offered 'a chance to ensure an increase in transparency around the tax affairs of potential suppliers of government contracts [and] the opportunity to ensure the exclusion of companies that have engaged or are engaging in egregious tax abuse';[22] this time namechecking 'Amazon collecting public money through large and rapidly growing government IT contracts, while the tax payments of this company remain opaque'.[23] Yet another contributor asked: 'with a British company paying full British tax versus one … which pays no tax, does the overall cost of that service become less for the one paying tax? It seems the Minister's

from: https://hansard.parliament.uk/lords/2022-07-11/debates/B1AC0 045-EDC1-4A84-B6BC-4B301BB673C2/ProcurementBill(HL) [Accessed 23 February 2024].

[21] Procurement Bill [HL], volume 823, debated on Monday 11 July 2022, Lord Wallace of Saltaire, column 341GC, Available from: https://hans ard.parliament.uk/lords/2022-07-11/debates/B1AC0045-EDC1-4A84-B6BC-4B301BB673C2/ProcurementBill(HL) [Accessed 23 February 2024].

[22] Procurement Bill [HL], volume 824, debated on Monday 24 October 2022, Lord Hunt of Kings Heath, column 278GC, Available from: https://hansard.parliament.uk/lords/2022-10-24/debates/87250 434-8ABA-40F5-89C3-C1A3E4D5B5F7/ProcurementBill(HL)#contr ibution-8E86E492-3B33-4EE6-95AE-05EF42F51003 [Accessed 23 February 2024].

[23] Procurement Bill [HL], volume 824, debated on Monday 24 October 2022, Lord Hunt of Kings Heath, column 279GC, Available from: https://hansard.parliament.uk/lords/2022-10-24/debates/87250 434-8ABA-40F5-89C3-C1A3E4D5B5F7/ProcurementBill(HL)#contr ibution-8E86E492-3B33-4EE6-95AE-05EF42F51003 [Accessed 23 February 2024].

answer is that the tax take is not included in the calculation of value for money.'[24]

Therefore, the new UK public procurement legislation clearly comes at a time of considerable concern that when public services are being outsourced, often this results in public resources, via these contracts, being channelled away from the state, where they might be deployed in the public interest, and into the pockets of private investors in corporations without delivering public value in return. The worry is that the delivery of public services via outsourced arrangements has become an exercise of value extraction.

Aim of the book

Reflecting on these developments, this book is written from the perspective of a corporate lawyer concerned with internal governance rules in corporations – broadly understood here as any organization that is incorporated – which, in turn, are directly implicated by their corporate *ownership* structure. We use 'ownership' in this context as a shorthand for the legal design of a bundle of rights, set out in the firm's constitution and in corporate law, that determines the parameters for how the corporation will be governed (further discussed in Chapter Four). Beneficiary rights derive from rules that set the organization's corporate purpose and define the fiduciary duties of directors,

---

[24]   Procurement Bill [HL], volume 824, debated on Monday 24 October 2022, Baroness Neville-Rolfe, column 289GC, Available from: https://hans ard.parliament.uk/lords/2022-10-24/debates/87250434-8ABA-40F5-89C3-C1A3E4D5B5F7/ProcurementBill(HL)#contribution-8E86E 492-3B33-4EE6-95AE-05EF42F51003 [Accessed 23 February 2024]. See also Crerar, P. (2022) 'One in six UK public procurement contracts had tax haven link, study finds', *The Guardian* [online], 24 September, Available from: www.theguardian.com/politics/2022/sep/24/one-in-six-uk-public-procurement-contracts-had-tax-haven-link-study-finds [Accessed 23 February 2024].

determining whose interests they are meant to prioritize. Related, control rights describe the allocation of decision-making power and accountability within the organization, whereas economic rights are defined by rules determining the distribution and sharing of profits in the organization, and the extent of any constrains on their distribution.

In the UK's default version of a commercial company limited by shares, these elements currently prioritize shareholders – those holding the company's equity. The purpose of the company, reflected in the legal fiduciary duties of its directors, prioritizes shareholders' interests. While directors take control of day-to-day governance of the company, shareholders have important intervention rights, including to appoint and dismiss the directors. Share price appreciation and dividend payments provide shareholders (but not other stakeholders) with a return on the company's profits. By conferring these privileges on shareholders, the company legal form has the advantage of enabling the business to attract equity investment and access capital in the pursuit of growth, to diversify its assets or expand by acquiring other companies. But where the company delivers public services on behalf of the state, this design can increase governance problems insofar as it enables companies to operate a financialized corporate model that prioritizes the maximization of profit and shareholder returns even above the long-term sustainability of the firm and its stakeholders or, more to the point, over their partnership with the state. While company law does not mandate this ownership model *per se*, the current default rules, by prioritizing shareholders, still do relatively little to prevent firms from choosing to maximize value extraction and short-term returns on investment.[25]

---

[25] See, generally, Ireland, P. (1999) 'Company law and the myth of shareholder ownership', *The Modern Law Review*, 62(1): 32-57.

Currently, the state, in outsourcing public services, transfers considerable public resources to an extractive corporate ownership model, reflected in the kind of organizations discussed in the Lords exchanges provided earlier. This, however, risks that these very providers deplete the state's own resources further by extracting value from these public contracts whenever they can, with the result that, eventually, the state's dependency on private delivery may be reinforced. From a wider economic policy perspective, this sort of arrangement, especially when it goes on repeatedly and over a long period of time, sustains financialized corporations in extractive ownership, even if these organizations are not contributing to an economically, socially and environmentally sustainable economy. Public service outsourcing, in other words, becomes an endorsement of and funding mechanism for unsustainable and financialized market actors.

The question I explore in this book is whether, by integrating more sustainable forms of corporate ownership into public outsourcing, we can instead create a positive and mutually reinforcing dynamic in the partnership between public and private contracting parties that improves service delivery and supports a sustainable economy. The internal governance of corporate organizations in sustainable ownership – where beneficiary, control and economic rights are reconfigured 'away' from the investor-centric default model to reflect economic, environmental and social sustainability objectives – is potentially more aligned with the governance objectives of the public actors they contract with. It is this closer alignment which may improve the governance of public services by reducing problems related to value extraction in their delivery. At the same time, such an arrangement nurtures more sustainable market actors by giving them better access to public markets, providing funding and room to grow or become economically sustainable. I see the potential for a win-win, a positive feedback loop that both improves the public outsourcing relationship and avoids more financialization in the wider economy. Again, debates in the Lords reflect at least some of these sentiments in suggesting that

> there is and should be a significant role for [the non-profit] sector alongside profit-making outsourcing companies and government agencies, particularly in th[e] sensitive area of personal social public services. We support a mixed economy in the provision of public services, not an overwhelming dependence on large outsourcing contractors regardless of the type of service provided.[26]

One Lords member even proposed that for personalized services in particular, it would be appropriate 'to get rid of all financialized provision and see it all in non-profit hands'.[27]

The traditional non-profit sector, however, is not the only alternative to financialized provision, nor arguably should we be limiting our focus, in proposing more sustainable forms of corporate ownership in contractual delivery, to personalized care services. Indeed the governance model I am investigating in this book could reach considerably further, potentially into any area where complex public service contracts are operating, and encompass a variety of sustainable corporate ownership forms, going beyond traditional non-profits. This may include, for example, purpose-driven companies which are run for

---

[26] Procurement Bill [HL], volume 823, debated on Monday 11 July 2022, Lord Wallace of Saltaire, column 341GC, Available from: https://hansard.parliament.uk/lords/2022-07-11/debates/B1AC0045-EDC1-4A84-B6BC-4B301BB673C2/ProcurementBill(HL) [Accessed 23 February 2024].

[27] Procurement Bill [HL], volume 823, debated on Monday 11 July 2022, Baroness Bennett of Manor Castle, column 342GC, Available from: https://hansard.parliament.uk/lords/2022-07-11/debates/B1AC0045-EDC1-4A84-B6BC-4B301BB673C2/ProcurementBill(HL) [Accessed 23 February 2024].

profit but also commit in their articles of association to wider social purposes and governance. The writer and *Guardian* columnist Will Hutton would be a proponent of this sort of position. He has recently proposed the creation of a new category of 'public benefit company' in Britain that would 'write into its constitution that its purpose is the delivery of public benefit to which profit-making is subordinate. For instance, a water company's purpose would be to deliver the best water as cheaply as possible and not siphon off excessive dividends through a tax haven.'[28] A similar proposal appeared recently in a leaked correspondence from the chief executive officer of one of the UK's troubled private water providers. It talked of the 'repurposing' of utilities providers 'into a new breed of declared social purpose companies – companies that remain privately owned, who absolutely can (and should) make a profit, but ones that also have a special duty to take a long-term view'.[29] Going beyond these proposals, there are also, as I hope to demonstrate in this book, possibilities for experimentation and development of different other sustainable corporate ownership forms in public service outsourcing.

Such proposals will not be uncontroversial. They might involve a limiting of competition for some public tenders that may cause concern, at least initially. But the problems in currently existing outsourcing arrangements are serious, and alternative solutions, drawing on contractual or regulatory governance instruments or even public ownership, are neither

---

[28] Hutton, W. (2018) 'We can undo privatisation. And it won't cost us a penny', *The Guardian* [online], 9 January, Available from: www.theguard ian.com/commentisfree/2018/jan/09/nationalise-rail-gas-water-privat ely-owned [Accessed 26 February 2024].

[29] Lawson, A. (2023) 'Severn Trent chief proposes "social purpose" water firms amid utilities crisis', *The Guardian* [online], 30 June, Available from: www.theguardian.com/business/2023/jun/30/severn-trent-chief-social-purpose-water-firms-utilities-crisis-liv-garfield-thames-water-lab our-renationalisation [Accessed 26 February 2024].

ideal nor cost-free. In this wider context, to co-opt sustainable corporate ownership forms into outsourcing relationships, to improve both public services and the wider economy, does seem an important inquiry worth pursuing, in research and policy. This does not, it is important to clarify, amount to advocating a particular normative position on whether more or less outsourcing of public services is desirable or indeed feasible. The premise of this book is normatively neutral on this position – if anything, it considers public service outsourcing, and the need for partnership between private and public actors to grow capacity to deliver complex welfare services, as a fact of modern economic and political life. But the discussion also recognizes that different interventions, including insourcing (taking more services back into public ownership), are available to address current problems in public service outsourcing. The point is to acknowledge the benefits of outsourcing but encourage a 'rethink' to improve both its functioning and the wider operation of our economies, a solution that does not advocate 'more market' or 'more state' but a realignment in the organization of, and partnership between, the market and the state. The book, in its detailed discussions, focuses on the UK position and frameworks, but the themes are also valid outside the UK given that public outsourcing trends elsewhere are not dissimilar. Therefore, while the book remains focused on the UK context in terms of its policy proposals, I hope, in the more general sections of this book, to highlight their relevance elsewhere too.

Structure of the book

Chapter One introduces primary and secondary objectives in public service outsourcing. While the former focus on the delivery of the services in question, the latter address the pursuit of ancillary policy goals in their delivery – for example, to create employment and new businesses, to address discrimination and inequalities, and to support environmentally sustainable business practice. In line with the aims of the book, the chapter considers secondary objectives that relate to corporate ownership forms, introducing the new duty in UK law to consider business diversity in public procurement as well as current policies that support smaller and social providers in public procurement. The chapter considers, more generally, the evolution of 'social value' as a secondary procurement objective in Britain.

Chapter Two outlines typical problems in current public service outsourcing. Complex public contracts are inevitably incomplete, leaving gaps and ambiguities, and allowing discretion in their delivery, which contracting parties may exploit for their benefit. Exploitation becomes particularly problematic where the state relies repeatedly on private partners, creating risks of incumbency and lock-in effects that can give rise to dependencies, transferring capacity from the public to the private sector, sometimes permanently (in the form of institutional knowledge, for example). Where private suppliers operate a financialized governance model, incentives to exploit both incomplete contracting and incumbency situations are further reinforced.

Chapter Three surveys a range of governance interventions that are available for states to resolve outsourcing problems. Contractual governance centres on improving contract design and management, seeking to strike a balance between detail and formalized contracting and relational or framework contracts. Beyond contracting, the state may seek leverage in public markets (public procurement) to impose accountability on providers keen to enter or continue their partnership with the public sector, or it may, by selecting different types of provider, diversify its provider pool to temper incumbency powers. It may use regulatory governance to impose additional constraints on providers, supplementing contractual and market mechanisms, and it may potentially create an institutional body – for example, a public or regulatory agency – to oversee implementation.

Chapter Four examines solutions to public outsourcing problems that rely on changes to supplier ownership. These include, on the one hand, the possibility of insourcing public services – taking them back in-house – to reinstate public ownership. Public ownership comprises variations beyond traditionally centralized administrative control, including, for example, the majority state-owned company. But, on the other hand, the state may select private providers that commit to a sustainable corporate ownership form in which internal governance elements relating to purpose (beneficiary rights), power (control rights) and profit (economic rights) are reconfigured so as to temper financialization within the firm, ensuring that the governance incentives of public and private contracting partners align more closely and reducing the risk of exploitation and formalization of outsourcing contracts.

Chapter Five explores the design elements in sustainable ownership: corporate purpose, power and profit. It introduces designs in social economy organizations but also those that operate in the wider economy. In the social economy, these encompass community interest companies, cooperative or community benefit societies and companies limited by guarantee operating under a non-distribution constraint. Those in the wider economy include purpose-driven firms that distribute profits, including certified B Corps or firms incorporated (outside the UK) as a benefit corporation. The chapter considers stakeholder co-determination and mutual and employee-owned firms as well as companies in foundation ownership. It provides no comprehensive survey but addresses what these forms of sustainable corporate ownership might be able to offer to improve public service outsourcing and reduce existing problems and failures.

Chapter Six considers that by outsourcing more services to sustainably owned suppliers, the state can create important secondary benefits in terms of strengthening the role of these organizations in the economy while also improving public service outsourcing. Winning public contracts can help these organizations access finance and build other important resources (such as governance and measurement tools) to sustain and grow their business, to innovate, to diversify and to reward their workers. There is potential for a positive feedback loop in which the state can create win–win by reducing outsourcing risks at the same time as nurturing more sustainable market actors, tempering the wider problems of a financialized corporate economy for society.

Chapter Seven assesses the potential design of a new procurement policy on sustainable corporate ownership, which would likely be permissive, leaving scope for discretion and experimentation with bidders mapping themselves against the criteria of sustainable ownership (purpose, power, profit). It considers how the policy might be accommodated within the current legal framework for procurement, assuming, given its very recent introduction, that appetite for further legislative changes will be limited, at least in the short term. The chapter considers both reserved contracting procedures and award criteria relating to quality and to wider social value. Substantively, the policy would have to be assessed carefully against a number of risks, including its potential impacts on competition and capabilities in service delivery and on existing social economy organizations. These, however, are not intransigent problems in the medium term.

Finally, the Conclusion briefly summarizes the overall argument of the book.

ONE

Outsourcing Public Services

Primary objectives

Where the state decides that the market cannot provide certain goods or services in sufficient quantities or quality, or in a sufficiently just distribution, it considers whether to take political responsibility for their provision as a public service. This includes, most obviously, security, education and healthcare, but also potentially other essentials like transport, water, energy and electronic and postal communications. In deciding whether to assume any particular responsibility, it determines the public need and the opportunity costs of meeting this need as a public service, balanced against other priorities and the quantity, quality and distribution of the same goods or services by the market. Whether and to what extent it should intervene is a political choice for which it must be accountable politically.

The extent of these political choices varies. In healthcare, for example, the US model historically encourages markets in health insurance and healthcare services, while European states tend to take political responsibility for health as a public service as part of a state-funded system. How these choices evolve is not always linear or predictable. A change in political leadership or an external trigger like a global crisis can bring about sudden shifts. For example, COVID-19 caused many governments to take on unprecedented levels of responsibility for the provision of healthcare equipment and services. Conversely, the global financial crisis in 2008 led many states to shed responsibilities to rein in spending.

Just because the state assumes responsibility for a service does not mean that it must become the provider. It also decides whether to deliver the service directly (in-house) or to contract for its delivery by private actors (outsourcing), usually through some form of competitive tendering process (public procurement). We can understand this decision through the lens of discretion and agency. Many of these services are highly complex. They necessitate discretion in delivery that cannot be efficiently assumed centrally and is, then, necessarily delegated to agents. By selecting either a public or private delivery model, the state determines who should exercise that discretion and what form of governance regime to impose on them.

Opting for in-house delivery, the state hands discretion to public officials, who are subject to the oversight of a public administrative governance regime with an emphasis on administrative procedure to ensure public sector organizations directly deliver public services efficiently.[1] The details depend on how the state organizes its public administration; this can range from a centralized bureaucratic hierarchy to a decentralized public management structure. When the state outsources, it confers some discretion over the delivery of the service to private providers, with oversight by a private mode of governance.[2] The state swaps the direct control it exerts over in-house providers for a contractual governance mechanism.[3] While it remains accountable under public law doctrines that secure the 'substantive legality and procedural

---

[1] Dunleavy, P. (1991) *Democracy, Bureaucracy and Public Choice: Economic Explanations in Political Science*, Abington: Routledge.

[2] Stringham, E.P. (2015) *Private Governance: Creating Order in Economic and Social Life*, Oxford: Oxford University Press.

[3] Vincent-Jones, P. (2000) 'Contractual governance: institutional and organizational analysis', *Oxford Journal of Legal Studies*, 20(3): 317–351.

regularity of government action',[4] these do not automatically apply to the private providers. Instead, accountability depends on the effectiveness of the contract as a governance tool, and on the capacity of the state to design and manage contracts and tender procedures, which may be enhanced by additional public governance mechanisms.

The choice between public and private delivery involves a complex range of economic and political considerations, not least whether the state should fill an identified capacity gap in-house or by turning to private providers. Even when the state theoretically has the in-house resources to fill a capacity gap, it must still decide whether this is the best use of its capacity or whether outsourcing would be a better option as it would free it to do other things. More detailed factors will also impact on its choices, including the character and geographical reach of the service, the delivery time frame, how demand fluctuates and its capacity to manage outsourced provision, as well as structural aspects of public administration like the availability of collaboration between different public bodies.[5] In the UK framework, important central decisions on the delivery of a public service require 'an analytical, evidenced-based' delivery model assessment,[6] which is based on a value for money criterion generally defined as a 'judgment about the optimal use of public resources to achieve stated objectives'.[7] Ultimately, it

---

[4] Freeman, J. (2003) 'Extending public law norms through privatization', *Harvard Law Review*, 116(5): 1285–1352, p 1302.

[5] Bovaird, T. (2016) 'The ins and outs of outsourcing and insourcing: what have we learnt from the past 30 years?', *Public Money and Management*, 36(1): 67–74.

[6] HM Government (2023) *The Sourcing Playbook* [online], June, p 20, Available from: https://assets.publishing.service.gov.uk/media/64901 fcc5f7bb700127fac5e/Sourcing_Playbook_Final.pdf [Accessed 26 February 2024].

[7] HM Treasury (2022) *The Green Book: Central Government Guidance on Appraisal and Evaluation* [online], June, p 52, Available from: www.gov. uk/government/publications/the-green-book-appraisal-and-evaluat ion-in-central-governent [Accessed 26 February 2024]. HM Treasury

is all about whether the public sector or the private sector can most effectively, efficiently and equitably deliver the service. Getting that decision right frees up resources that can be used elsewhere.[8] Of course, many of the choices around the quality, cost and distribution of public services are political, as is the time horizon for assessing the costs and benefits.

Most states, like Britain, mix public and private delivery, and have significantly increased privatization in recent decades, with this now extending to nearly every type of public services. Underpinning the trend has been an assumption – sometimes justified – that markets can do things better; they can direct resources more effectively and efficiently to where they are needed and extend the capacities of the state. That assumption does not mean the state has *necessarily* reduced its ambition to provide welfare – to 'shrink' its responsibilities. It might also sometimes outsource to 'buy in' additional capacity from the private sector to deliver more ambitious public services. Outsourcing enables the state to integrate private actors into the delivery of goods and services in order to strengthen its capabilities to deliver public services that meet its political promises. It increases the choice of provider and extends who can influence the design and resourcing of public services rather than leaving this to the determination of a limited number of public sector organizations with fixed budgets and bureaucratic structures. As well, private actors can bring flexibility that public agencies sometimes struggle to provide. For example, private suppliers are often not limited by the same political restrictions or geographical boundaries that impact public authorities, lending them an agility that secures economies of

---

(2023) *Managing Public Money* [online], May, Available from: https://ass ets.publishing.service.gov.uk/media/65c4a3773f634b001242c6b7/Man aging_Public_Money_-_May_2023_2.pdf [Accessed 26 February 2024].

[8] Freeman, J. (2003) 'Extending public law norms through privatization', *Harvard Law Review*, 116(5): 1285–1352, p 1296.

scale and scope. Given constraints on public capabilities, this might prove essential where, without outsourcing, the state lacks the resources to deliver ambitious welfare programmes. Once it has made the political choice to provide a public service, private delivery might, in these situations, be the only way for the state to find the resources to follow through on that choice, at least in the required time frame.

By tendering contracts for the delivery of public services to the market, the state imposes competitive pressure on providers to reduce costs and raise service quality to win contracts. If done well, this can deliver efficiencies and innovation that state bureaucracies struggle to provide, especially in rapidly scaling to meet an accelerated demand, since maintaining state capacity during extended periods of low demand can tie up public resources inefficiently.[9] Outsourcing can help the public sector to become more efficient and even eventually enable it to bring the services back in-house.[10] A successful tendering can also force transparency where partners must expose the value and outcomes of individual service elements in the contracting document rather than 'bury' them in, for example, public charters or budget documents.[11]

Of course, a private delivery model demands public resources too, albeit not necessarily of the same type or from the same public authority as in-house provision. Managing large public tenders and complex, sometimes long-term public contracts

---

[9] Williamson, O.E. (2005) 'The economics of governance', *American Economic Review*, 95(2): 1–18, p 11.

[10] Sasse, T., Nickson, S., Britchfield, C. and Davies, N. (2020) *Government Outsourcing: When and How to Bring Public Services Back into Government Hands* [online], Institute for Government, June, p 6, Available from: www.instituteforgovernment.org.uk/sites/default/files/publications/gov ernment-outsourcing-public-services-government-hands.pdf [Accessed 23 February 2024].

[11] Bovaird, T. (2016) 'The ins and outs of outsourcing and insourcing: what have we learnt from the past 30 years?', *Public Money and Management*, 36(1): 67–74.

requires investment in organizational structures and skilled personnel, for which the public sector competes with market actors. Once a service is outsourced, it is essential for the state to retain enough capabilities within the public sector to potentially step back in as provider. Decisions on whether to insource or outsource therefore always involve balancing a number of public capabilities against each other, including the ability to provide a service directly, or to ensure the state can potentially step back in, and the resources required to tender, manage and monitor public contracts effectively. In that respect, while contracting may be more efficient for delivering relatively simple goods and services, in-house provision may be better suited for the delivery of more complex and long-term services that require some joined-up thinking and need different public agencies to collaborate where necessary.[12]

An important factor in determining efficiencies in outsourcing contracts is the time frame that contracting authorities apply in weighing costs and benefits of the contract and, related to this, whether they assess quality in addition to price when selecting private partners. In practice, by investing in a delivery model that considers more than the cheapest available price, the state may harness greater benefits in the long term. Where public resources are scarce, however, contracting authorities are more likely to focus on tightly defined unit costs and short-term efficiencies. In practice, it can be easier for the state, for political reasons or as a result of economic pressures in a context of public austerity, to select those who it can safely assert will have the capacity and the skills to save money in the short term and to select providers on price over quality, even if this is likely to come at a high price in the long term. Some risk aversity is to be expected, not least

---

[12] Hart, O. (2003) 'Incomplete contracts and public ownership: remarks, and an application to public-private partnerships', *Economic Journal*, 113(486): C69–C76.

because these questions are often professionally significant for public managers. As governments adopt outsourcing decisions with significant but deferred effects, they are unlikely to be held accountable for them immediately, which means that they can even potentially exploit, for their own political gain, short-term decisions, delegating difficult delivery choices relating to, for example, reductions in service levels or cost savings. A long-term approach to contracting efficiencies, on the other hand, acknowledges that the benefits of private delivery are often not static targets that the state can set out to 'achieve' as soon as outputs are delivered. Inevitably, especially when contracting for complex services, these benefits bear a dynamic quality relating to a range of long-term outcomes. Although the state's contractual commitments are always time specific, it can encourage long-term dynamic efficiency – for example, by involving a range of private providers to create vibrant public markets that deliver services sustainably – over the static efficiency of contracting always with the cheapest.

Secondary objectives

States often outsource to achieve secondary objectives beyond the primary objectives of effective, efficient and equitable provision of the public service. The secondary objective may be some macroeconomic aim or industrial policy, perhaps to create jobs during a period of unemployment, to invest in the skills of the state's workforce with training and apprenticeship schemes, to address issues of discrimination, to redistribute to areas in need of regeneration or to reorient the economy towards a strategic objective, like the 'net zero' target, and build industrial capacity around it. Here, the state, in addition to using public money to deliver a public service via outsourcing, incorporates obligations into the contract which relate to an ancillary objective, thus tying the private actors involved into promoting the ancillary objective as well as delivering the service. Historically, the use of 'policy-led' public procurement is long-standing.[13] Perhaps most famously, Roosevelt's New Deal public works programmes dealt with mass unemployment and destitution in the US after the Great Depression triggered by the 1929 stock market crash. In Britain too, 'government procurement has a long history as a social policy mechanism, wherein the 1980s to 2014 period of commercial dominance in procurement policy [effectively, from Thatcherism and New Labour through to the enactment of new EU public procurement legislation in 2014] represents the anomaly'.[14]

The use of secondary policies creates an issue for public procurement law and policy – fundamentally, raising questions of whether to restrict, to permit, to encourage or even to compel their use. And despite its long-standing history, substantive debates continue over how far contracting authorities may, or indeed should, use their public contracting powers to pursue ancillary objectives.[15] Some distinguish, in the context of these debates, between the state's function as purchaser and its use of public contracting as a regulatory tool to implement secondary policies, replacing or supplementing the use of more traditional regulatory instruments (for example, labour law or environmental law).[16] Views differ on how permissive or

---

[13] Harland, C.M. (2021) 'Policy-led public procurement: does strategic procurement deliver?', *Journal of Public Procurement*, 21(3): 221–228.

[14] Hamilton, S.G. (2022) 'Public procurement – price-taker or market-shaper?', *Critical Perspectives on International Business*, 18(4): 574–615, p 579.

[15] Arrowsmith, S. and Kunzlik, P. (eds) (2009) *Social and Environmental Policies in EC Procurement Law: New Directives and New Directions*, Cambridge: Cambridge University Press. Arrowsmith, S. (2010) 'Horizontal policies in public procurement: a taxonomy', *Journal of Public Procurement*, 10(2): 149–186. Sanchez-Graells, A. (ed) (2018) *Smart Public Procurement and Labour Standards: Pushing the Discussion after RegioPost*, Oxford: Hart Publishing.

[16] Arrowsmith, S. and Kunzlik, P. (2009) 'Public procurement and horizontal policies in EC law: general principles', in S. Arrowsmith and P. Kunzlik (eds) *Social and Environmental Policies in EC Procurement Law: New Directives and New Directions*, Cambridge: Cambridge University Press, pp 9–54.

restrictive a policy and legal procurement regime should be on these issues. While a permissive regime would widen the state's autonomy to implement regulatory choices contractually, a restrictive regime would limit this flexibility. These are political choices reflected in the relevant laws and policies under which contracting authorities, and the public sector generally, will be held accountable. A permissive perspective would insist that the state may exercise its preferences as purchaser just like in any private market (for example, the freedom of the purchaser to choose environmentally friendly products over others). This perspective may also give particular importance to accountable public actors to express these preferences, as long as they are transparent. In fact, 'some see the role of government as being in part to represent the collective preferences of citizens [and] when the government buys purchases, it acts in the name of its citizens and ought to uphold certain standards.'[17] The counterposition generally 'derives from a concern that the adverse effects of [secondary objectives in procurement] outweigh any good that may come of them' – for example, because they increase costs of procurement, reduce transparency, lead to more bureaucracy and increase the risk of corruption or of reduced competition.[18] This restrictive position, then, considers that incorporating a secondary purpose into public contracts can introduce complexity and uncertainty – and ultimately inefficiency – into the delivery of the public contract. Where contracts try to simultaneously achieve a multiplicity of goals, some of which can be in tension,

---

[17] McCrudden, C. (2007) 'Corporate social responsibility and public procurement', in D. McBarnet, A. Voiculescu and T. Campbell (eds) *The New Corporate Accountability: Corporate Social Responsibility and the Law*, Cambridge: Cambridge University Press, pp 93–118, p 97.

[18] McCrudden, C. (2007) 'Corporate social responsibility and public procurement', in D. McBarnet, A. Voiculescu and T. Campbell (eds) *The New Corporate Accountability: Corporate Social Responsibility and the Law*, Cambridge: Cambridge University Press, pp 93–118, p 103.

they potentially become more difficult to specify. Secondary objectives can then erect entry and regulatory barriers, creating a division between public and private markets for comparable services and, by limiting competition for public contracts, reducing the market's ability to create efficiencies.[19]

Where procurement policy and law reflect a restrictive position, they will generally tend to limit contracting authorities' ability to select providers on anything other than economic criteria. This approach applied, for example, when compulsory competitive tendering was effective for UK local authorities and under earlier iterations of the current EU public procurement legislation which the UK implemented too. The current UK regime however is, subject to certain restrictions, more permissive. It encourages and, more recently, even compels some contracting authorities to consider, and even more specifically to apply, secondary objectives. The turning point in the UK regime came partly as a result of the shifting priorities in EU public procurement law which opened up greater flexibilities to apply secondary objectives, first marginally in 2004 and then more substantially from 2014. After initially taking a restrictive view on secondary policies, the EU has gradually accepted their use and in certain limited situations even requires them.[20] In addition, the introduction

---

[19] Sanchez-Graells, A. (2015) *Public Procurement and the EU Competition Rules* (2nd edn), Oxford: Hart Publishing, pp 39 et seq. Sanchez-Graells, A. (2016) 'Truly competitive public procurement as a Europe 2020 lever: what role for the principle of competition in moderating horizontal policies?', *European Public Law*, 22(2): 377–394. Sanchez-Graells, A. (2018) 'Regulatory substitution between labour and public procurement law: the EU's shifting approach to enforcing labour standards in public contracts', *European Public Law*, 24(2): 229–254.

[20] European Commission (2010) *Europe 2020: A Strategy for Smart, Sustainable and Inclusive Growth*, COM(2010) 2020 final [online], p 12, Available from: www.eea.europa.eu/policy-documents/com-2010-2020-europe-2020 [Accessed 8 April 2024]. European Commission (2015) *Study on 'Strategic Use of Public Procurement in Promoting Green, Social and*

of new UK legislation from 2012 that expressly introduced the consideration of 'social value' into public procurement for some contracts moved the dial further towards a permissive stance on secondary policies.[21]

Secondary policies can be woven into public contracting in a variety of ways and at different stages. Contracting authorities may, for example, wish to strategically exclude from the tendering process those providers who fall short of certain characteristics that align with the ancillary objectives in question. In fact, the 2004 EU public procurement directives introduced for the first time a requirement for Member States to use public contracts to support a secondary purpose by excluding from certain contracts providers with convictions for corruption, certain forms of fraud, money laundering or participation in a criminal organization. Similar grounds for mandatory or discretionary exclusion have over time been extended, including in the new UK legislation (though some would argue this has not gone quite far enough). It is also in principle possible under the current regime, in certain circumstances and mainly for smaller procurements, for contracting authorities to reserve (or 'set aside') public contracts for providers that align with secondary policies that the authority determines are important.[22]

Innovation Policies', Final Report, DG GROW, Luxembourg: Publications Office of the European Union.

[21] Public Services (Social Value) Act 2012. Boeger, N. (2017) 'Reappraising the UK social value legislation', *Public Money and Management*, 37(2): 113–124.

[22] Sanchez-Graells, A. (2015) *Public Procurement and the EU Competition Rules* (2nd edn), Oxford: Hart Publishing, pp 301 et seq. The literature on this aspect is vast across jurisdictions – see, for example: Bates, T. (2015) 'Contested terrain: the role of preferential policies in opening government and corporate procurement markets to black-owned businesses', *Du Bois Review: Social Science Research on Race*, 12(1): 137–159; Orser, B., Riding A. and Weeks, J. (2019) 'The efficacy of gender-based federal procurement policies in the United States', *International Journal of*

An example would be the reservation of contracts for local businesses.[23]

Alternatively, in selecting successful tenders, contracting authorities may choose to (or indeed be compelled to) integrate secondary objectives into the criteria they apply when evaluating the capability of bidders or the respective merit of their bids. In this, the introduction of social value criteria in the UK has, from the passing of legislation in 2012, had significant impact. That law requires public authorities, including local and central government as well as NHS commissioning bodies and housing associations, to consider the 'economic, social and environmental well-being of the relevant area' before they procure major public service contracts.[24] The government has developed detailed further-reaching guidance on and models of how to apply social value.[25] It has recently introduced a mandatory expectation that social value must be explicitly evaluated (as opposed to merely considered) in

---

Gender and Entrepreneurship, 11(1): 6–37; Hawkins, T., Gravier, M. and Randall, W.S. (2018) 'Socio-economic sourcing: benefits of small business set-asides in public procurement', *Journal of Public Procurement*, 18(3): 217–239.

[23] Cabinet Office (2020) *Procurement Policy Note – Reserving Below Threshold Procurements*, Action Note PPN 11/20 [online], December, Available from: https://assets.publishing.service.gov.uk/media/614c9c0fe90e077a2 e2adc44/20210923-PPN-11_20-Reserving-Below-Threshold-Procu rements.docx.pdf [Accessed 26 February 2024].

[24] Section 1(3) Public Services (Social Value) Act 2012.

[25] Government Commercial Function (2020) *The Social Value Model* [online], December, Available from: https://assets.publishing.service.gov. uk/media/5fc8b7ede90e0762a0d71365/Social-Value-Model-Edn-1.1- 3-Dec-20.pdf [Accessed 26 February 2024]. Government Commercial Function (2020) *Guide to Using the Social Value Model* [online], December, Available from: https://assets.publishing.service.gov.uk/media/5fc8b804d 3bf7f7f53e5a503/Guide-to-using-the-Social-Value-Model-Edn-1.1-3- Dec-20.pdf [Accessed 26 February 2024]. HM Government (2023) *The Sourcing Playbook*, June, p 62, Available from: https://assets.publishing. service.gov.uk/media/64901fcc5f7bb700127fac5e/Sourcing_Playbook_ Final.pdf [Accessed 26 February 2024].

all central government procurement, applying a minimum weighting of 10 per cent of the total score in the evaluation, insofar as requirements are proportionate and related to the subject matter of the contract.[26] In addition, the new UK public procurement legislation now imposes on contracting authorities, for the majority of public procurements, an expectation to have regard to a national public procurement statement which, in turn, lists certain social value outcomes that they should consider (see further Chapter Seven).[27] The documentation is detailed and other initiatives have grown around it, nationally and internationally, in both the private and public sectors, all seeking to capture, measure and support the generation of social value. Based on its development over the past decade or more, some now describe the UK's social value framework as a 'system' that has developed organically, made up of 'standards, rules and approaches that are often voluntary and depend upon the engagement of public bodies, private companies and practitioners'.[28] There are benefits

---

[26] HM Government (2020) *Procurement Policy Note – Taking Account of Social Value in the Award of Central Government Contracts*, Action Note PPN 06/20 [online], September, pt 2 and 12, Available from: https://assets.publishing.service.gov.uk/government/uploads/system/uploads/attachment_data/file/921437/PPN-06_20-Taking-Account-of-Social-Value-in-the-Award-of-Central-Government-Contracts.pdf [Accessed 26 February 2024].

[27] Section 13(9) PA2023. Cabinet Office (2021) *Procurement Policy Note – National Procurement Policy Statement*, Action Note PPN 05/21 [online], June, pt 10, Available from: https://assets.publishing.service.gov.uk/media/60b0c01d8fa8f5488e618b93/PPN_05_21-_National_Procurement_Policy_Statement.pdf [Accessed 26 February 2024].

[28] Social Enterprise UK (2023) *The Social Value 2032 Roadmap* [online], June, p 7, Available from: www.socialenterprise.org.uk/seuk-report/the-social-value-roadmap/ [Accessed 11 March 2024]. See also Nicholls, J. (2023) *The Future of Social Value in the United Kingdom* [online], Social Enterprise UK, Available from: www.socialenterprise.org.uk/seuk-report/the-future-of-social-value-in-the-united-kingdom/ [Accessed 13 March 2024].

in its organic development, as this has created room for experimentation and, for example, the dynamic development of social value measurement tools. But this has also led to weaknesses in that the system is relatively disjointed, lacking in communication and coherence and, therefore, often unaccountable in terms of whether social value commitments are genuinely met.[29] Some have criticized the UK legislator for not incorporating explicit references to social value into the new UK procurement legislation.[30]

Most secondary objectives directly target the *behaviour* of public service providers in the delivery of the contract – for example, their ability to offer additional employment opportunities or to protect environmental standards while supplying the goods or services in question. Likewise, the Organisation for Economic Co-operation and Development (OECD) promotes the idea of 'integrating responsible business conduct in public procurement', specifically by asking businesses to address broader issues like supply chain treatment when they contract with the public sector.[31] Not only procurement experts consider these issues important; corporate lawyers, too, acknowledge their potential. Sjåfjell, for example, proposes that a sustainability report be required from private companies as a prerequisite of

---

29 Social Enterprise UK (2023) *The Social Value 2032 Roadmap* [online], June, p 9, Available from: www.socialenterprise.org.uk/seuk-report/the-social-value-roadmap/ [Accessed 11 March 2024].

30 Social Enterprise UK (undated) *House of Commons Public Bill Committee Procurement Bill: Call for Evidence* [online], Available from: https://bills.parliament.uk/publications/49626/documents/2862#:~:text=However%2C%20the%20Procurement%20Bill%20s,is%20currently%20not%20universally%20implemented [Accessed 27 February 2024].

31 OECD (2020) *Integrating Responsible Business Conduct in Public Procurement* [online], Available from: www.oecd-ilibrary.org/sites/02682b01-en/index.html?itemId=/content/publication/02682b01-en [Accessed 9 April 2024].

participating in a public tender, using public procurement law as an enforcement mechanism to make companies pursue sustainable governance.[32]

Some secondary objectives, however, relate to their business form or corporate ownership structure. The 2021 national procurement policy statement, for example, lists 'improving supplier diversity' as both a social value outcome and a national priority outcome that contracting authorities should consider.[33] This implies that the state is concerned not only about how providers supply services in the pursuit of both primary and secondary objectives but also – as a secondary objective in and of itself – about ensuring a degree of diversity in the types of organization that supply them. Supporting different forms of corporate ownership – arguably an important aspect of 'supplier diversity' – is here seen as a public benefit in its own right.

A similar point is quite apparent in the UK government's recent initiatives to support the role of SMEs. SMEs, of course, do not represent a distinct corporate ownership form – they are, for the most part, smaller commercial companies or partnerships. Yet being smaller in scale and embedded in a local economy has, according to government,

[32] Sjåfjell, B. (2016) 'Sustainable public procurement as a driver for sustainable companies? The interface between company law and public procurement law', in B. Sjåfjell and A. Wiesbrock (eds) *Sustainable Public Procurement under EU Law: New Perspectives on the State as Stakeholder*, Cambridge: Cambridge University Press, pp 182–205.

[33] HM Government (2021) *National Procurement Policy Statement* [online], June, pt 10 and 13, Available from: https://assets.publishing.service.gov.uk/government/uploads/system/uploads/attachment_data/file/990289/National_Procurement_Policy_Statement.pdf [Accessed 26 February 2024]. Cabinet Office (2021) *Procurement Policy Note – National Procurement Policy Statement*, Action Note PPN 05/21 [online], June, pt 6 and 10, Available from: https://assets.publishing.service.gov.uk/media/60b0c01d8fa8f5488e618b93/PPN_05_21-_National_Procurement_Policy_Statement.pdf [Accessed 26 February 2024].

a distinct and beneficial effect on their governance and potentially a positive impact on their delivery. Here, it is worth quoting the Crown Commercial Service's summary in full:

> There are many benefits of working with SMEs such as good customer service, due to highly skilled and experienced workforces and smaller chains of command. SMEs are often more adaptable and agile to situations than larger organisations due to their smaller nature, which allows them to respond quickly and flexibly to changing requirements and provide the most suitable solution (ideal for tight timescales).
>
> SMEs can also support greater localisation, which can reduce carbon footprints associated with delivery helping to support public sector organisations in reaching net zero. They also create local jobs, and can contribute to the local social value agenda in other ways, as they are more committed to the community they live and work in.[34]

At the same time, however, the Crown Commercial Service also considers them to play a particularly important role in achieving quite a separate national priority outcome (thus, a secondary procurement objective in its own right) which in the 2021 national procurement policy statement is referred to

---

[34] Crown Commercial Service (2023) 'Levelling the playing field: the benefits of working with SMEs and how public sector organisations can make it easier for them to bid for work – procurement essentials' [online], updated 30 August, Available from: www.crowncommercial.gov.uk/ news/levelling-the-playing-field-the-benefits-of-working-with-smes-and-how-public-sector-organisations-can-make-it-easier-for-them-to-bid-for-work-procurement-essentials#:~:text=SMEs%20are%20the%20b ackbone%20of,working%20with%20the%20public%20sector [Accessed 26 February 2024].

as 'creating new businesses, new jobs and new skills'.[35] SMEs are, according to the Crown Commercial Service, seen as 'the backbone of any healthy economy: they drive growth, provide employment opportunities and open new markets'.[36] Nurturing their role by enabling better access to valuable public contracts, which allows them to grow and develop, in other words, creates win–win not only by improving service delivery (through efficiency and localization) but also by expanding secondary objectives (the benefits of a strong and diverse economy) in public outsourcing.

There is evidence too of this same win–win rationale in policies to support the role of voluntary, community and social enterprises (VCSEs) in public procurement. VCSEs represent not one but a variation of corporate ownership models, from cooperative and mutual ownership to social enterprises – often equated with civil society or the 'third sector'. What unites them is that being committed to a social purpose, they are quite distinct from traditional commercial ownership (their characteristics and implications are further discussed in

[35] HM Government (2021) *National Procurement Policy Statement*, June, pt 10 and 13, Available from: https://assets.publishing.service.gov.uk/governm ent/uploads/system/uploads/attachment_data/file/990289/National_ Procurement_Policy_Statement.pdf [Accessed 26 February 2024]. Cabinet Office (2021) *Procurement Policy Note – National Procurement Policy Statement*, Action Note PPN 05/21 [online], June, pt 6 and 10, Available from: https://assets.publishing.service.gov.uk/media/60b0c 01d8fa8f5488e618b93/PPN_05_21-_National_Procurement_Policy_ Statement.pdf [Accessed 26 February 2024]. Section 13(9) PA2023.

[36] Crown Commercial Service (2023) 'Levelling the playing field: the benefits of working with SMEs and how public sector organisations can make it easier for them to bid for work – procurement essentials' [online], updated 30 August, Available from: www.crowncommercial.gov.uk/ news/levelling-the-playing-field-the-benefits-of-working-with-smes-and-how-public-sector-organisations-can-make-it-easier-for-them-to-bid-for-work-procurement-essentials#:~:text=SMEs%20are%20the%20b ackbone%20of,working%20with%20the%20public%20sector [Accessed 26 February 2024].

Chapter Four). The important point here is that the VCSE Crown representative describes these VCSE ownership models as, on the one hand, playing

> a crucial role in our journey of transforming how the government delivers smarter, more thoughtful and effective public services that meet the needs of people across the country … [providing] place-based solutions [that] can create a greater impact for those most in need, who are hard for the traditional public sector to reach

while at the same time highlighting their contribution 'to economic growth, making the economy more innovative, resilient and productive'.[37] These two distinct benefits – namely, improving service delivery (localized, thoughtful and effective services) while at the same time supporting a more innovative, resilient and productive economy – can be mutually reinforcing: by supporting one we can also nurture the other. There is, once again, the possibility of win–win.

---

[37] Department for Digital, Culture, Media, and Sport (2022) *The Role of Voluntary, Community, and Social Enterprise (VCSE) Organisations in Public Procurement* [online], August, p 3, Available from: https://assets.publishing.service.gov.uk/government/uploads/system/uploads/attachment_data/file/1100749/The_role_of_Voluntary__Community__and_Social_Enterprises_in_public_procurement.pdf [Accessed 26 February 2024].

TWO

Problems in Public Service Outsourcing

Incomplete contracts

Once the state chooses to outsource public services, the outsourcing instrument – usually a public or concession contract – becomes the key mechanism for the extension of public control over their private delivery. The success of outsourcing then 'hinges on the viability of the outsourcing contract as a fully effective junction of instruction' between public authority and private provider.[1] But given the complexity of many public services, the contractual governance mechanism has some inevitable limitations. Bar perhaps in the simplest procurement of public goods, it is quite impossible or impossibly costly to anticipate all contingencies and service obligations in detail in the contracting instrument.[2]

---

[1] Innes, A. (2018) *First-Best-World Economic Theory and the Second-Best-World of Public Sector Outsourcing: The Reinvention of the Soviet Kombinat by Other Means*, LEQS Paper No 134/2018 [online], London School of Economics and Political Science, May, p 2, Available from: www.lse. ac.uk/european-institute/Assets/Documents/LEQS-Discussion-Papers/ LEQSPaper134.pdf [Accessed 26 February 2024].

[2] Williamson, O.E. (1979) 'Transaction-cost economics: the governance of contractual relations', *Journal of Law and Economics*, 22(2): 233–261, p 237. Hart, O., Shleifer, A. and Vishny, R. (1997) 'The proper scope of government: theory and an application to prisons', *Quarterly Journal of Economics*, 112(4): 1127–1161, p 1133. Lonsdale, C. (2005) 'Contractual

Certain contingencies are unpredictable (such as a natural disaster or economic crisis), and others are difficult to foresee (such as unexpected or unaccounted needs).[3] Yet other elements are ambiguous precisely because they relate to quality-related service standards that are non-contractible, as is often the case in relation to personalized services – as in the care sector, where services rely heavily on qualities such as maintaining a sense of patients' personal dignity, trust between patients and carers, and continuity of care.[4] These often depend on standards that relate to organizational values as much as the more tangible conditions of their delivery, such as the employment conditions of carers. While the latter can at least potentially be specified in a public contract to some extent, the former are harder to define and enforce contractually. This poses a double challenge of predicting both contingencies and how a specific provider might react to them.

Given the incomplete nature of complex public contracts, the need for adaptation will arise as gaps and ambiguities in the contract emerge. Ideally, the contracting parties will fill these out by informally renegotiating their relationship without negatively impacting the quality of service delivery. But an important factor to consider in this context is that successful adaptation can be considerably more difficult in the case of

uncertainty, power and public contracting', *Journal of Public Policy*, 25(2): 219–240.

[3] Maskin, E. and Tirole, J. (1990) 'Unforeseen contingencies and incomplete contracts', *The Review of Economic Studies*, 66(1): 83–114.

[4] Bergman, M., Lundberg, S. and Spagnolo, G. (2012) *Public Procurement and Non-Contractible Quality: Evidence from Elderly Care* (Umeå Economic Studies 846) [online], Umeå University, Available from: http://sh.diva-portal.org/smash/get/diva2:809601/FULLTEXT02.pdf [Accessed 10 April 2024]. Maskin, E. (2002) 'On indescribable contingencies and incomplete contracts', *European Economic Review*, 46(4–5): 725–733. Domberger, S. and Jensen, P. (1997) 'Contracting out by the public sector: theory, evidence, prospects', *Oxford Review of Economic Policy*, 13(4): 67–78, p 71.

public contracts compared to private contracts. The reason lies not in any distinction related to scale or complexity, nor in how much uncertainty there is to tackle, or in what form. On these issues, private and public contracts give rise to broadly similar difficulties. What is different is the typical incentive structures in the contracting relationship.

The state enters an outsourcing contract in the pursuit of a public interest, for which it is responsible under a system of political and public administrative accountability. As provider of last resort, it is subject to public accountability for the delivery of public services and takes on extensive long-term risks and liabilities should the contractual delivery fail. The private service provider, on the other hand, is typically motivated by an economic choice that will be determined by its organizational context. Speaking broadly, the state has an undeniable systemic and long-term commitment to the delivery of the public service, while the provider's commitment is often primarily transactional and focused on the short or medium term. The public contract therefore incorporates a set of potentially conflicting public and private incentives, especially when the selected provider is a commercially operating private organization, such as a for-profit company or partnership. The state's overall incentive in the contracting relationship is to manage the contract to ensure delivery and to discharge its public obligations (and avoid liability in public law) on terms that reflect a public interest, foremost being the cost-effective use of public money. For the private contractor, the incentive is to price its services appropriately and organize their delivery in order to serve the purpose, interests and priorities of its own economic organization (which, of course, may differ from case to case).

In circumstances of conflicting incentives between public and private contracting parties, informal renegotiation of contractual obligations, if the need arises, is difficult. An important concern for the state, seeking to serve the public interest, in these situations is the question of how far it can rely on providers to fill any gaps and ambiguities in the same way that it would have done had it been able to anticipate and pre-specify these at the time of entering into the contract. Where the provider is a commercial organization, it is only to be expected that its management will respond to contractual uncertainty by exploiting it for the benefit of the commercial interests of the organization. Managers will ensure that the organization complies with regulatory or contractual constraints to the extent that they consider it in the best interest of the members or partners not to incur fines or not to sully the firm's reputation. But, putting the firm's economic interest first, they will be tempted to exploit contractual ambiguities for profit where it is possible to do so – for example, by shirking some of their obligations, by overcharging or underdelivering, by holding up the public sector to increase profits where renegotiation is necessary or by refusing to renegotiate. They may insist on the text of the contract, and doing so allows the private contractor to gain an advantage (to appropriate a rent), and potentially a large enough advantage to outweigh any potential losses from a breakdown and early termination of the contractual relationship. For the public sector, these strategies lead to rising transaction costs in the form either of expensive renegotiation or enforcement action or of contracting failure that may even force the state to re-tender services or take them back in-house.[5]

Contract management then becomes a zero-sum game between the state and the private provider: the further the latter pulls one way, seeking to exploit uncertainties and ambiguities for private gain, the more the state must pull back by drafting contracts more specifically (with greater complexity), tightening performance measurement and contract monitoring and, if necessary, complaints procedures or

---

[5]   Williamson, O.E. (2005) 'The economics of governance', *American Economic Review*, 95(2): 1–18, p 15.

in extreme cases, punitive measures that include the possibility of excluding providers from future tenders. In these situations, the relationship between the public and private partners, which should be marked by mutual reliance and cooperation, can instead become highly formalized.[6] But resolving contractual ambiguities or unexpected risks by way of formal renegotiation or, if necessary, judicial interpretation is both costly and time-consuming.[7]

Incumbency

Once a public contract is awarded, the relationship between state and provider becomes an asset which both can have an incentive to hold on to (see Box 2.1). For the provider, this is typically because it is profitable to do so. For the state, holding on to the provider, even if it means repeatedly awarding contracts to them, can have advantages too. For example, the state might be inclined to establish a closer relationship with certain larger and more established suppliers to help improve efficiencies for large outsourcing projects and generate a mutual understanding with important partners that may be justified as a safe and effective choice. These suppliers can, for instance, be expected to 'bring economies of scale and expertise; they can be less likely to suffer corporate failure and they can have the financial resilience to absorb upfront

6   Beuve, J., Moszoro, M. and Saussier, S. (2019) 'Political contestability and contract rigidity: an analysis of procurement contracts', *Journal of Economics & Management Strategy*, 28(2): 316–335.

7   For an example, see *BT Cornwall Ltd v Cornwall Council & Ors* [2015] EWHC 3755 (Comm). See also Vincent-Jones, P. (1997) 'Hybrid organisation, contractual governance and compulsory competitive tendering in the provision of local authority services', in S. Deakin and J. Michie (eds) *Contracts, Co-Operation and Competition: Studies in Economics, Management and Law*, Oxford: Oxford University Press, pp 143–174, p 154.

costs. They can also help to manage long supply chains of smaller providers.'[8]

These considerations have led the UK government to implement a regime for selecting a group of commercial companies as 'strategic suppliers', whose relationship with the government is centrally coordinated by the Cabinet Office as part of its responsibility to promote efficiency in public procurement, and whose role as public suppliers is deemed strategically important. The list currently comprises about forty businesses. In principle, there is no guarantee a firm will stay on it long term, because suppliers are removed if their public sector revenue decreases or, more dramatically, if a company fails. But, in practice, some large providers have been on the list for several years. Typically, the government spends over £100 million per year on outsourced goods and services with each of these strategic suppliers. For these companies, becoming a strategic supplier can therefore be lucrative even if means trading the benefits of closer access to key procurement officials within government against the burden of some increased monitoring and scrutiny.

But incumbency can become a problem where public outsourcing decisions are repetitive and the public sector habitually selects specific private providers, often as repeat players, leading to forms of adverse selection.[9] Market

---

8   National Audit Office (2013) *The Role of Major Contractors in the Delivery of Public Services*, presented to the House of Commons on 12 November 2013 [online], pt 11, Available from: www.nao.org.uk/wp-content/uploads/2013/11/10296-001-BOOK-ES.pdf [Accessed 26 February 2024]. National Audit Office, *Lessons Learned: Competition in Public Procurement*, presented to the House of Commons on 19 July 2023 [online], Available from: www.nao.org.uk/wp-content/uploads/2023/07/lessons-learned-competition-in-public-procurement.pdf [Accessed 26 February 2024].

9   'Only six of the 40 [strategic suppliers in 2022] had not been reprimanded by regulators, with many receiving tens of millions in fines without losing their place as a strategic supplier' – Kersely, A. (2023) 'Firms fined most by regulators still on UK government's list of top suppliers', *The*

concentration means these organizations can eventually become too big or too important to fail, accumulating important resources like information and data which the state relies on in the long term.[10] By resorting to a relatively small pool of private contractors over time, the state leaves potentially high entry barriers for others – for example, where tendering procedures and contract specifications are easier for larger or incumbent providers to navigate. Under these conditions, the opportunities for these existing providers in exploiting gaps and ambiguities in incomplete public contracts for their own strategic benefit, and at the expense of public resources, are considerable. Problems of opportunism and rent-seeking are reinforced because a limited choice makes switching providers more difficult or costly for the state. This only strengthens the hand of existing providers where contracts need to be renegotiated to accommodate contingencies and changes, such as cost overruns, including in cases of strategically underpriced bids. In these situations, where private providers are placed in a relationship of heightened bargaining power vis-à-vis the public sector, ensuring that the delivery of the public service is managed in the public interest and not for the financial benefit of the private provider can become impossible or exceedingly

Guardian [online], 23 May, Available from: www.theguardian.com/polit ics/2023/may/28/firms-fined-most-by-regulators-still-on-uk-governme nts-list-of-top-suppliers [Accessed 26 February 2024].

[10] In terms of market concentration, strategic suppliers in 2021–2022 earned the equivalent of 11 per cent (or £19 billion) of overall public sector spending on outsourcing contracts even though they represented only 0.3 per cent of all public sector suppliers – Tussell (2022) *UK Strategic Suppliers: 2022 Interim Report* [online], May, Available from: www.tussell. com/hubfs/Tussell%20-%20UK%20Strategic%20Suppliers%202022%20 Interim%20Report.pdf?utm_medium=email&_hsmi=212908582&_ hsenc=p2ANqtz-_lwWb6YOSthbQHF47pTTap2GYOgsniN-0uE5n Tc_-BypdN0YJxcPsG9ETX6YX37fLFEwH5IpuqhBigRbwcjBrAC2n kBg&utm_content=212908582&utm_source=hs_automation [Accessed 26 February 2024].

costly.[11] In the UK, these concerns are reinforced by a lack of transparency regarding financial data and profits. Compared to other jurisdictions, the UK has one of the most protective approaches to non-disclosure of commercially sensitive information in the context of public procurement governance and litigation.[12] And the use of early warning clauses in public contracts, such as 'living will' obligations that help flag when an existing provider is in financial distress, are currently considered good practice but not mandatory.[13]

Extensive and repeated outsourcing in multiple sectors and over long periods reinforces these problems (see also Box 2.1). The concrete risk is that following extended periods of privatization, resources are drawn away from the public sector and reinvested, indirectly through public contracting, in the private sector or simply lost. However, this means that over time the capability of the public sector itself is being eroded, forcing the state increasingly to buy in private sector capacity, including for tasks that it might otherwise have

---

[11] National Audit Office (2013) *Managing Government Suppliers*, presented to the House of Commons on 12 November [online], p 14, Available from: www.nao.org.uk/wp-content/uploads/2013/11/10298-001-Governments-managing-contractors-HC-811.pdf [Accessed 26 February 2024]. House of Commons Committee of Public Accounts (2018) *Strategic Suppliers* [online], 24 July, Available from: https://publications.parliament.uk/pa/cm201719/cmselect/cmpubacc/1031/1031.pdf [Accessed 26 February 2024].

[12] Henty, P. and Ashmore, R. (2019) 'Disclosure rules within public procurement procedures and during contract period in the United Kingdom', in K.-M. Halonen, R. Caranta and A. Sanchez-Graells (eds) *Transparency in EU Procurements: Disclosure within Public Procurement and during Contract Execution*, Cheltenham: Edward Elgar, pp 296–322.

[13] HM Government (2023) *The Sourcing Playbook* [online], June, p 20, Available from: https://assets.publishing.service.gov.uk/media/64901fcc5f7bb700127fac5e/Sourcing_Playbook_Final.pdf [Accessed 26 February 2024].

chosen to keep in-house.[14] Path dependencies are created as long-term public capabilities are depleted precisely because public contracts absorb the funds that could otherwise be used to generate and maintain in-house capacity. These effects can then only be stopped and reversed with significant levels of additional investment, which might be too difficult or politically unpopular to mobilize. At some point, public sector capacity might be reduced by such an extent that the state is locked into a private delivery mode, and it then becomes very difficult to take services back in-house without, at least, a longer transition period and/or expensive reinvestment. But in a scenario of depleted public capabilities post privatization, particularly when combined with politically driven economic austerity, a trimmed down public sector is hardly in a strong position to manage complex contractual arrangements in a way that can shield the public interest from, for example, strategic exploitation by private providers.

A particular difficulty rests in guaranteeing the availability and continued access to the valuable resources of information, data and knowledge that usually come with being involved directly in the delivery of a public service. With outsourcing, these resources are handed over and made accessible to the private sector, risking asymmetries that mean suppliers hold more relevant information, and build up more relevant skills, than the state over time due to the displacement of institutional memory and increased control over relevant data associated with the delivery of the public service. Again, these dynamics are impacted by limitations on transparency for the benefit of commercial secrecy and as a result of the fact that the freedom of information regime applies to public agencies but often

---

[14] National Audit Office (2017) *Capability in the Civil Service*, presented to the House of Commons on 24 March 2017 [online], Available from: www.nao.org.uk/wp-content/uploads/2017/03/Capability-in-the-civil-service.pdf [Accessed 10 April 2024].

does not apply to private organizations providing contracted services.[15] They can result in lock-in effects, particularly where public services rely on proprietary technological solutions.[16] These resources are usually very difficult for the public sector to replenish (and *if* it is possible to do so, this is expensive). They may be permanently lost unless concrete institutional structures are put in place to control and secure continuing access to them for public institutions. The UK government could, for example, significantly develop its initiatives for documented and systematic institutional memory capture from suppliers to achieve a proper and comprehensive understanding of the ways in which they manage and deliver public services. This might enable it to decouple the necessary knowledge base and institutional memory from the current provider (as well as its management and workforce), averting a permanent loss of information from the public sector to private institutions.[17]

The state will face these consequences when it considers re-internalizing a service after a period of outsourcing – for example, when political circumstances or public needs change – or a specific outsourcing arrangement is perceived

---

[15] Information Commissioner's Office [undated] *Transparency in Outsourcing: A Roadmap* [online], Available from: https://ico.org.uk/media/1043531/transparency-in-outsourcing-roadmap.pdf [Accessed 26 February 2024]. Information Commissioner's Office (2019) *Outsourcing Oversight? The Case for Reforming Access to Information Law*, Report of the Information Commissioner to Parliament [online], Available from: https://ico.org.uk/media/about-the-ico/documents/2614204/outsourcing-oversight-ico-report-to-parliament.pdf [Accessed 26 February 2024].

[16] Matuszewska-Pautsch, K. (2020) ' "Vendor lock-in" in IT contracts – what to consider when choosing and using IT systems', *Public Procurement Law Review*, 29(1): 1–15.

[17] Government Commercial Function (2021) *Resolution Planning: Guidance Note* [online], May, Available from: https://assets.publishing.service.gov.uk/media/60a388c7e90e07356f0fdd30/Resolution_planning_guidance_note_May_2021.pdf [Accessed 26 February 2024].

to be faulty. They impact particularly where the state has to adapt welfare capacities quickly in response to urgent demand for public intervention and coordinated mobilization of public and private resources (the recent COVID-19 pandemic being an example at hand). To keep enough resilience in the public sector to respond effectively to such sudden shocks and manage long-term developments, the state must maintain the flexibility to switch, when necessary, from one delivery model to another relatively quickly so that it can unlock additional public resources and avoid lock-in effects by ensuring public services can be taken back in-house without prohibitive cost or administrative barriers. If these public resources are not protected, extended reliance on the private sector profoundly diminishes the state's long-term capabilities to provide public welfare, 'infantilizing' the public sector by making it dependent on external skills and resources.[18]

Box 2.1

Serco, a strategic government supplier and FTSE 250 listed multinational company, was found to be deliberately overcharging the Ministry of Justice for several years in the delivery of public contracts for electronic tagging of offenders.[a] In 2019, the company settled fraud charges for doing so.[b] Reportedly, Serco executives deliberately inflated the company's costs by a significant margin – including for the tagging of offenders who the company did not actually monitor, some of whom had returned to prison or were deceased – in invoices submitted to the Ministry of Justice, after realizing that the company's profit margins were far higher than it had expected when it tendered for the contract.[c] Serco's chief executive has acknowledged that reforms

---

[18] Dunhill, L. and Syal, R. (2020) 'Whitehall "infantilised" by reliance on consultants, minister claims', *The Guardian* [online], 29 September, Available from: www.theguardian.com/politics/2020/sep/29/whiteh all-infantilised-by-reliance-on-consultants-minister-claims [Accessed 26 February 2024]. See also Mazzucato, M. and Collington, R. (2023) *The Big Con*, London: Penguin.

in the company's management control systems, internal audit and management assurance processes were necessary to avoid similar failings in future.[d]

Despite these failures in its past, Serco continues to successfully operate as key provider of large public contracts. Although the tagging scandal led to a temporary freeze in Serco bidding for government contracts, it has resumed its position as one of the largest UK strategic suppliers and recently delivered key contracts under the NHS COVID-19 'test and trace' programme, controversially choosing to resume dividend payments as a result of a significant growth in profits from these contracts.[e] The government's award of public contracts for setting up and running a test and trace system during the pandemic is itself emblematic of large-scale outsourcing failure. The total investment (not just to Serco, but overall) in these contracts amounted to £37 billion over two years, yet the Public Accounts Committee review in 2021 found it 'had not achieved its main objective' despite these 'eye watering' costs.[f] The committee concluded especially that the system's over-reliance on private consultants would be 'likely to cost taxpayers hundreds of millions of pounds', with average daily rates of £1,100, potentially equating to over £1 million a day.[g] According to the National Audit Office, the ten top consultancies under test and trace had accrued contracts to the value of £300 million by 2021. The largest share went to the big accountancy firm Deloitte, followed by other multinational consultancies.[h] Serco, meanwhile, proceeded to subcontract large parts of its own contractual obligations under test and trace to a group of subcontractors and initially refused to reveal their details on account of commercial sensitivity.[i] Reportedly among them were private firms which had themselves been previously involved in significant failures in different service outsourcing contracts.[j]

a Travis, A. (2013) 'Offender tagging: Serco to repay more than £68m in overcharging', *The Guardian*, [online] 19 December, Available from: https://www.theguardian.com/business/2013/dec/19/offender-electronic-tagging-serco-repay-68m-overcharging [Accessed 26 February].

b Press Association (2019) 'Serco fined £22.9m over electronic tagging scandal', *The Guardian*, [online] 3 July, Available from: https://www.theguardian.com/business/2019/jul/03/serco-fined-229m-over-electronic-tagging-scandal [Accessed 26 February 2024].

c Jolly, J. (2021) 'Ex-Serco executives discussed inflating costs on tagging contracts, papers show', *The Guardian*, [online] 28 April, Available from: https://www.theguardian.com/business/2021/apr/28/serco-tagging-contracts-serious-fraud-office-trial [Accessed 26 February 2024].

d   Ministry of Justice (2019) 'SFO Investigation of Serco and G4S Government Contracts', Letter from Robert Buckland QC MP, Minister for Justice, to Bob Neill MP, Chair, Justice Select Committee, House of Commons, 3 July [online], Available from: https://www.parliament.uk/globalassets/documents/commons-committees/Justice/SFO-investigation-Serco-G4S-contracts.pdf

e   Sweney, M. (2021) 'Labour calls Serco's decision to pay millions to investors 'outrageous', *The Guardian*, [online] 25 April, Available from: https://www.theguardian.com/business/2021/feb/25/serco-to-pay-first-divid end-in-seven-years-after-profits-double   [Accessed 26 February 2024]. On the size of Serco's contracts see Norris, A. MP (2021) 'NHS Test and Trace: Serco - Question for Department of Health and Social Care',13 September [online], Available from: https://questions-statements.parliament.uk/written-questions/detail/2021-05-13/1190/   [Accessed 26 February 2024].

f   House of Commons Committee of Public Accounts (2021) 'Test and Trace update' [online] 27 October, Available from: https://committees.parliament.uk/publications/7651/documents/79945/default/ pp 3 and 5 [Accessed 26 February 2024].

g   House of Commons Committee of Public Accounts (2021) 'Test and Trace update' [online] 27 October, Available from: https://committees.parliam ent.uk/publications/7651/documents/79945/default/ p 7 [Accessed 26 February 2024]. Gregory, A. (2021) 'England's Covid test and trace spending over £1m a day on consultants', *The Guardian*, [online] 21 November, Available from: https://www.theguardian.com/world/2021/nov/21/england-covid-test-and-trace-spending-over-1m-a-day-on-consultants   [Accessed 26 February 2024].

h   National Audit Office (2021) 'Test and Trace in England – Progress Update, June [online], Available from: https://www.nao.org.uk/wp-content/uploads/2021/06/Test-and-trace-in-England-progress-update.pdf, p 45 [Accessed 26 February 2024]. Foy, S. (2021) 'Inside Deloitte's role in the UK's 'eye-wateringly' expensive test and trace disaster', *The Telegraph*, [online] 28 December, Available from: https://www.telegraph.co.uk/business/2021/12/28/inside-deloittes-role-uks-eye-wateringly-expensive-test-trace/. [Accessed 26 February 2024].

i   Information Commissioner's Office (2021) 'Reference: IC-83975-T5P4 Freedom of Information Act 2000 (FOIA)Decision notice', [online] 7 October, Available from: https://ico.org.uk/media/action-weve-taken/decision-noti ces/2021/4018727/ic-83975-t5p4.pdf [Accessed 26 February 2024].

j   Johnston, J. (2021) 'Exclusive: Serco Subcontracted NHS Test And Trace Work To Firm Accused Of "Meltdown" On Government Call Centre Contract', *PoliticsHome*, [online] 5 February, Available from: https://www. politicshome.com/news/article/exclusive-serco-subcontracted-test-and-trace-work-to-firm-accused-of-meltdown-on-government-call-centre-contract [Accessed 26 February 2024]. Lister, S. and Dearden, L. (2018) 'Tax credit claimants who suffered from botched Concentrix outsourcing plan paid just £14 compensation each', *The Independent*, [online] 21 January, Available from: https://www.independent.co.uk/news/uk/politics/tax-cred its-concentrix-scandal-cut-compensation-14-hmrc-scandal-outsourc ing-privatisation-a8170246.html [Accessed 26 February 2024]. Johnston, J. (2020) 'Exclusive: Serco Have Subcontracted Contact Tracing Jobs To The Company Embroiled In The Tax Credits Scandal And Debt Collection Companies', *PoliticsHome*, [online] 22 September, Available from: https:// www.politicshome.com/news/article/serco-contract-tracing-concent rix [Accessed 26 February 2024]. Staton, B. (2019) 'Outsourcing of duty solicitors suffers call centre 'meltdown'', *The Financial Times*, [online] 29 August, Available from: https://www.ft.com/content/9e39d590-ca6b-11e9-a1f4-3669401ba76f [Accessed 28 February 2024].

Issues in corporate governance

The internal governance of the service provider can exacerbate problems in incomplete outsourcing contracts and incumbency situations. Reflected in recent outsourcing failures is a *pattern* of value extraction whereby managers of key suppliers, because they are running corporations with a financialized governance model, aggressively implement short-term strategies that prioritize their own interests and those of their investors over the public interest or indeed that of any other stakeholders, including suppliers, customers or employees, to the point where their behaviour becomes reckless in the pursuit of profit. It is a governance model that has been vividly described by one parliamentary committee as marked by 'hubris and greed ... a relentless dash for cash, driven by acquisitions, rising debt, expansion into new markets and exploitation of suppliers [with increased] dividend every year, come what may [while] obligations, such as adequately funding its pension schemes, [are] treated with contempt'.[19]

---

[19] House of Commons Business, Energy and Industrial Strategy and Work and Pensions Committees (2018) *Carillion* [online], 16 May, p 3, Available from: https://publications.parliament.uk/pa/cm201719/cmsel ect/cmworpen/769/769.pdf [Accessed 26 February 2024].

From the point of view of a contracting authority in a public outsourcing project, partnering with a corporate provider with a financialized governance model reinforces existing risks in incomplete public contracts and incumbency situations: their governance model renders these providers poised to exploit contractual ambiguities and gaps as well as any incumbency power they might hold, to further their own commercial interest. These providers' internal governance priorities to maximize profit mean that the organizational incentives of private and public partners are, in this constellation, *widely* misaligned to start with. In the search for greater efficiencies and access to private capital to boost public capabilities, the state, by relying on financialized corporate partners, therefore ends up potentially creating new transaction costs in having to bridge a widening 'governance gap' to ensure that these private providers do not exploit ambiguities or dependencies in public contracts to extract value when, by corporate design, they are set up to do just that in the pursuit of profit. The more it relies on these corporate actors to deliver public services, the more the state may have to intervene by imposing tighter external governance measures on them, ensuring that they do not exploit problems that arise from contractual incompleteness and situations of incumbency. Failing to do so risks the consequences of contracting failure.

Despite these risks, financialized corporations have, in recent years, gained public contracts in the most sensitive and complex areas of public welfare delivery, from prison services to social care, including as strategic suppliers that end up determining important aspects of the delivery of these public services.[20] Companies with hedge fund shareholdings win these contracts

---

[20] House of Commons Committee of Public Accounts (2018) *Strategic Suppliers* [online], 24 July, Available from: https://publications.parliam ent.uk/pa/cm201719/cmselect/cmpubacc/1031/1031.pdf [Accessed 26 February 2024]. Tussell (2022) *UK Strategic Suppliers: 2022 Interim*

while at the same time their investors are shorting shares and their executives are aggressively restructuring their corporate tax burden, leveraging debt on their companies and accelerating dividend payments to maximize shareholder returns even when it comes at the cost of delivering value for money. Recent patterns of extraction, and failure, also involve a growing role for private equity investment funds, often registered overseas, in acquiring ownership of firms that deliver privatized services on behalf of the public sector in Britain, as they 'look upon the public domain as an unexploited potential market'.[21] Acquisitions often involve high leveraging of target companies (see Box 2.2). Highly extractive and focused on the short term, their corporate governance strategies do little to strengthen the financial resilience and sustainability of the company supplying the public service in question, but instead create financial risks not unlike those in the much-publicized failure of the strategic supplier Carillion, a listed company.[22]

These strategies are enabled by the wider regulatory environment for corporate governance and international financial markets, including a relatively permissive framework

Report [online], May, Available from: www.tussell.com/hubfs/Tuss ell%20-%20UK%20Strategic%20Suppliers%202022%20Interim%20 Report.pdf?utm_medium=email&_hsmi=212908582&_hsenc= p2ANqtz-_lwWb6YOSthbQHF47pTTap2GYOgsniN-0uE5n Tc_-BypdN0YJxcPsG9ETX6YX37fLFEwH5IpuqhBigRbwcjBrAC2n kBg&utm_content=212908582&utm_source=hs_automation [Accessed 26 February 2024].

[21] Leys, C. (2001) *Market-Driven Politics*, London: Verso, p 213.

[22] House of Commons Business, Energy and Industrial Strategy and Work and Pensions Committees (2018) *Carillion* [online], 16 May, Available from: https://publications.parliament.uk/pa/cm201719/cmselect/ cmworpen/769/769.pdf [Accessed 26 February 2024]. Makortoff, K. (2023) 'KPMG settles £1.3bn lawsuit from Carillion creditors over alleged negligence', *The Guardian* [online], 17 February, Available from: www.theguardian.com/business/2023/feb/17/kpmg-pays-13bn- to-settle-negligent-auditing-claim-by-carillion-creditors [Accessed 26 February 2024].

of corporate and capital markets law, takeover legislation and the emergence of corporate governance codes that continue to prioritize the interests of shareholders. These frameworks reflect considerable deference by government to the financial interest of corporations.[23] For example, it chose not to strengthen capital maintenance rules to impose stricter control on excessive dividend payments or to restrict share buybacks, even after concerns were raised following the demise of Carillion that these practices had contributed to its failure.[24] It recently withdrew a legislative initiative that would have imposed tighter accountability, in the form of additional reporting obligations, on large companies relating to their financial resilience.[25] Likewise, the 2024 iteration of the UK's corporate governance code, which under the UK listing rules applies to all (domestic and foreign) companies with a premium listing on the London Stock Exchange on a 'comply or explain' basis, introduces only limited changes to strengthen the previous (pre-Carillion) version, clearly

---

[23] See generally Deakin, S. (2018) 'Reversing financialization: shareholder value and the legal reform of corporate governance', in C. Driver and G. Thompson (eds) *Corporate Governance in Contention*, Oxford: Oxford University Press, pp 25–41.

[24] According to parliamentary committees in 2018, 'Carillion's dividend payments bore little relation to its volatile corporate performance' – House of Commons Business, Energy and Industrial Strategy and Work and Pensions Committees (2018) *Carillion* [online], 16 May, p 17, Available from: https://publications.parliament.uk/pa/cm201719/cmselect/cmworpen/769/769.pdf [Accessed 26 February 2024].

[25] See draft Companies (Strategic Report and Directors' Report) (Amendment) Regulations 2023, withdrawn on 16 October 2023. Department for Business and Trade (2023) 'Corporate reporting: The Draft Companies (Strategic Report and Directors' Report) (Amendment) Regulations 2023', *Gov.uk* [online], updated 20 October, Available from: www.gov.uk/government/publications/new-transparency-over-res ilience-and-assurance-for-big-business/corporate-reporting-the-draft-companies-strategic-report-and-directors-report-amendment-regulati ons-2023 [Accessed 2 March 2024].

to avoid overprescription that might impact on financial interests.[26] The corporate governance system relies heavily on the role of non-executive directors and increasingly on provisions relating to corporate audit and reporting, to impose accountability on the boardroom. But it imposes hardly any further-reaching prescriptive regulation on executive directors. Key factors are the lack of effective regulatory intervention to control equity-based executive remuneration schemes and a relative absence in some key jurisdictions (including in the UK and the US) of stakeholder representation on company boards, as well as continuing shortcomings in the regulatory framework to ensure diversity on company boards more broadly.[27]

Finally, company law itself can act as enabler of financialized governance in corporations. The UK corporate legal framework, for example, defaults to a position that defines the fiduciary duty of the company directors in terms of promoting 'the success of the company for the benefit of its members as a whole' – that is, prioritizing its shareholders.[28] In so doing, directors are required to have regard to other stakeholders, including employees and customers, but this obligation is only procedural. It imposes on directors a duty to take a degree of care in their decision-making process with a view to considering factors that may impact on the long-term

---

[26] See Financial Reporting Council (2024) *UK Corporate Governance Code* [online], January, Available from: https://media.frc.org.uk/documents/UK_Corporate_Governance_Code_2024_kRCm5ss.pdf [Accessed 27 February 2024]. Institute of Directors (2024) 'IoD welcomes targeted changes to the UK Corporate Governance Code' [online], 22 January, Available from: www.iod.com/news/iod-welcomes-targeted-changes-to-the-uk-corporate-governance-code/ [Accessed 2 March 2024].

[27] On the latter, see Financial Conduct Authority (2022) *Diversity and Inclusion on Company Boards and Executive Management*, Policy Statement PS22/3 [online], April, Available from: www.fca.org.uk/publication/policy/ps22-3.pdf [Accessed 2 March 2024].

[28] Section 172(1) Companies Act 2006.

success of the business. But the law does not compel them to follow through on those considerations. If they conclude, for example, that prioritizing short-term shareholder interests by awarding dividends is what the business needs, company law would not penalize them. While encouraging an inclusive perspective, UK company law does not actively prevent an extractive governance design whereby directors simply maximize profit for shareholders – where, in other words, financialized governance reigns. Likewise, the current UK corporate governance framework imposes obligations of good governance on shareholders – incentivizing behaviour that amounts to good corporate 'stewardship' – mainly in the form of soft law expectations, rather than by imposing legal responsibilities.[29] From the perspective of a contracting authority, this design offers little reassurance that the supplier company will not act opportunistically where it is in the shareholders' interest to do so.

Box 2.2

In 2011, Southern Cross, at the time the largest private care home provider for the UK public sector and a FTSE listed company, collapsed after declaring itself unable to repay debts it had acquired to expand the company. The demise affected over 40,000 staff and services provided to over 30,000 care home residents in the UK.[a] Its reasons related to an earlier private equity buyout of the company followed by a 'sale and leaseback' strategy to finance its rapid expansion ahead of its initial listing in 2006. The acquisition of large debt rendered its business model unsustainable, leading to a rapid fall in share price after 2008 and its eventual demise.[b]

Many of the care homes owned by Southern Cross were sold to another large provider, Four Seasons Health Care. But in 2019, that company

---

[29] See Financial Reporting Council (2020) *The UK Stewardship Code 2020* [online], Available from: https://media.frc.org.uk/documents/The_UK_Stewardship_Code_2020.pdf [Accessed 26 February 2024].

collapsed too when income from its public contracts was not enough to provide care services and repay large debts it had taken on following a private equity acquisition and various refinancings.[c] As with the collapse of Southern Cross, the demise of Four Seasons affected many care home residents, reportedly more than it impacted the financial health of the private equity firm at the heart of the company.[d] Given that both Sothern Cross and Four Seasons were highly leveraged companies, Barbara Keeley, Shadow Minister for Social Care and Mental Health, reportedly pointed at the time to 'major concerns about the debt-driven business models of some companies in the care sector and the role of foreign private equity firms and hedge funds in deciding the future care arrangements for large numbers of vulnerable people'.[e] But these trends continue, as private equity funds are targeting investment in children's care homes despite concerns over failing service standards.[f] Among private childcare providers, a recent report 'found clear patterns of acquisitions and mergers and indebtedness'.[g]

a   Southern Cross Healthcare [HC], volume 529, debated on Tuesday 16 June 2011, Nick Smith MP, column 926, Available from: https://hansard. parliament.uk/Commons/2011-06-16/debates/11061639000006/Southern CrossHealthcare [Accessed 16 May 2024].

b   Curry, N. and Oung, C. (2021) 'Fractured and forgotten? The social care provider market in England', Nuffield Trust, April [online], pp 27–29, Available from: https://www.nuffieldtrust.org.uk/sites/default/files/2021-04/nuffield-trust-social-care-provider-market-web.pdf [Accessed 16 May 2024].

c   House of Commons Library (2019) 'Paper Four Seasons Health Care Group – financial difficulties and safeguards for clients, Briefing Paper [online] 5 November, Available from: https://researchbriefings.files.parliam ent.uk/documents/CBP-8004/CBP-8004.pdf [Accessed 26 February 2024].

d   Rowland, D. (2019) 'Corporate care home collapse and 'light touch' regulation: a repeating cycle of failure', LSE British Politics and Policy [Blog], 8 May, Available from: https://blogs.lse.ac.uk/politicsandpolicy/corporate-care-homes/ [Accessed 26 February 2024].

e   Davies, R. (2019), 'Four Seasons care home operator collapses into administration', The Guardian, [online] 30 April, Available from: https://www. theguardian.com/society/2019/apr/30/four-seasons-care-home-operator-on-brink-of-administration [Accessed 26 February 2024].

f   Aguilar García, C., Hunter-Green, Z. and Savag, M. (2023) 'Profiteering fears as global investment firms increase stakes in England's child social care', The Observer, [online] 23 December, Available from: https://www. theguardian.com/society/2023/dec/23/england-childrens-care-homes-backed-by-private-equity-firms-double-over-five-years [Accessed 16 May 2024]. For parliamentary debate, see Children's Care Homes: Private Equity [HL], volume 835, debated on Tuesday 30 January 2024, columns

1110–1113, Available from: https://hansard.parliament.uk/Lords/2024-01-30/debates/F1F07CB1-2B6A-4233-88F3-0C0E8026CDF7/Childr en%E2%80%99SCareHomesPrivateEquity [Accessed 16 May 2024]. McAlister, J. (2022) 'The independent review of children's social care – Final report', [online], May, Available from: https://assets.publishing.service. gov.uk/government/uploads/system/uploads/attachment_data/file/1141 532/Independent_review_of_children_s_social_care_-_Final_report.pdf [Accessed 26 February 2024].

g   Simon, A., Penn, H., Shah, A., Owen, C., Lloyd, E., Hollingworth, K. and Quy, K. (2022) 'Acquisitions, Mergers and Debt: the new language of childcare', *UCL Social Research Report*, [online] January https://discov ery.ucl.ac.uk/id/eprint/10142357/7/Childcare%20Main%20Report%20010 222.pdf, p 9 [Accessed 26 February 2024].

THREE

Solutions in Governance

Contracts

The state may reduce problems in public service outsourcing by designing governance solutions that impact directly on the public outsourcing relationship with a view to reducing exploitative and extractive behaviour. A starting point in developing these solutions is, once again, the public outsourcing contract, which offers the state direct (private) governance leverage over its private provider. To ensure that outsourcing delivers both primary and secondary objectives (see Chapter One), contracting authorities will want to optimize the effectiveness of the public contract as a governance tool. By ensuring that public contracts are drafted appropriately, the state can minimize the risk of exploitation, formalization and even unwanted dependencies. In practice, however, the decision of how to approach the drafting and management of public outsourcing contracts always involves a balancing of different factors, including complexity and resource intensity, intended and unintended effects, and choice between long-term and short-term perspectives. In particular, the state has a balance to strike between, broadly speaking, a relatively formal and detailed contract design and one that allows for greater flexibility and adjustment.

The state may try to anticipate and avoid conflict and exploitation of incomplete outsourcing contracts by introducing more detailed contractual provisions. It can introduce more detailed metrics and targets against which performance and outputs will be measured and assessed – for example, by strengthening the use of KPIs to measure performance, to make it both more difficult for providers to avoid obligations under the contract and easier for the public authority to hold providers to account during or at the end of the delivery. For large public contracts, the new public procurement legislation reinforces this by requiring contracting authorities, where possible, to set and publish at least three KPIs.[1] It runs a risk, however, that by designing overly complex contracts, the state expends public resources disproportionately without necessarily improving underlying issues related to, for example, power imbalances that can impact negatively on public contracting. The very conditions (for example, risk assurances, accounting requirements, clawback clauses) that are intended to hold providers to account and avoid exploitation can be those that are easier to address and absorb by larger and incumbent providers than smaller organizations and new entrants, thus undermining attempts at diversifying public service provision. And where detailed KPIs are poorly

---

[1]   Section 52 PA2023. The relevant threshold is an estimated contract value of £5 million. Exceptions apply in relation to certain contracts, including frameworks, utilities contracts, concessions or 'light touch' contracts, or if the contracting authority considers that the supplier's performance under the contract could not appropriately be assessed by reference to KPIs. They must, at least once every 12 months during the life cycle of the contract and on termination of the contract, assess and publish information on assessment against KPIs. See data on KPIs for government's most important contracts at: Cabinet Office (2020) 'Key Performance Indicators (KPIs) for government's most important contracts', *Gov.uk* [online], updated 25 January 2024, Available from: www.gov.uk/governm ent/publications/key-performance-indicators-kpis-for-governments-most-important-contracts [Accessed 27 February 2024]. Vara Arribas, G. (2021) 'The use of KPIs for exclusion on grounds of past performance in public contracts', *EIPA* [online], 12 March, Available from: www.eipa. eu/blog/the-use-of-kpis-for-exclusion-on-grounds-of-past-performa nce-in-public-contracts/ [Accessed 27 February 2024].

designed, unworkable or insufficiently robust, they can in fact create a source of dispute for contracting parties rather than a means of avoiding them.[2] Issues can arise particularly around the question of how much risk the provider will be required to absorb in delivering the contract. Aggressive risk transfer, such as asking suppliers to take on unlimited liability or demanding from smaller enterprises a parent company guarantee as mandatory insurance, can be a barrier to market entry and affect the treatment of subcontractors too.[3] The new public procurement legislation recognizes this by lifting requirements for suppliers to have pre-existing insurance before tendering for public contracts, which can be particularly onerous for SMEs.[4] But going further, these problems may affect larger suppliers too, and in the UK even 'large contracts have failed when government has transferred risks that suppliers have no control over and cannot manage, rather than those which suppliers can price and manage better than government'.[5]

To keep contracts manageable, the state may be tempted to draft performance clauses narrowly focusing on measurable outputs over wider outcomes that might be more long term or less easy to quantify. But again, there are risks that these

---

[2] Rhys-Jones, M. and Haugh, C. (2023) 'The Procurement Bill: key performance indicators and monitoring reforms explained', *Foot Anstey* [online], 29 June, Available from: www.footanstey.com/our-insights/artic les-news/the-procurement-bill-key-performance-indicators-and-mon itoring-reforms-explained/ [Accessed 27 February 2024].

[3] Pritchard, J. and Lasko-Skinner, R. (2019) *Please Procure Responsibly: The State of Public Service Commissioning* [online], Reform, March, Available from: https://reform.uk/wp-content/uploads/2019/04/Public-Serv ice-Procurement-web-version.pdf [Accessed 27 February 2024].

[4] Sections 22, 36, 37 and 46 PA2023.

[5] Sasse, T., Guerin, B., Nickson, S., O'Brien, M., Pope, T. and Davies, N. (2019) *Government Outsourcing: What Has Worked and What Needs Reform?* [online], Institute for Government, September, p 8, Available from: www. instituteforgovernment.org.uk/sites/default/files/publications/governm ent-outsourcing-reform-WEB.pdf [Accessed 27 February 2024].

strategies undermine rather than strengthen the effectiveness of the contractual tool. Over time, narrowly drafted contract specifications can create false economies, because they are unsuited to effectively preventing slipping service standards, especially of non-contractible or more complex service elements. In fact, rather than pre-empting ambiguities that might be exploited, the state might in reality set itself up to face exploitative behaviour from providers who, by insisting on previously agreed contractual terms, are justified in delivering services that turn out to be unsuited to meet complex public needs.[6] Given the state's long-term political responsibilities, this eventually forces the public sector to play a whack-a-mole game: one problem shifted now creates other problems elsewhere later, which in turn may require it to buy in further resources or re-internalize a service at significant additional cost in future, to address earlier failings in the delivery of welfare.

It is, on the other hand, to some extent possible with skilful drafting and contract management to avoid overly rigid contracting relationships by building room for adaptation and experimentation into outsourcing contracts, even at the risk of rendering their management more complex and less predictable.[7] This often means adopting a relational contract design where, recognizing the 'pressures to sustain ongoing

---

[6]   Vincent-Jones, P. (1997) 'Hybrid organisation, contractual governance and compulsory competitive tendering in the provision of local authority services', in S. Deakin and J. Michie (eds) *Contracts, Co-Operation and Competition: Studies in Economics, Management and Law*, Oxford: Oxford University Press, pp 143–174, p 154.

[7]   Classically, Macneil, I.P. (1978) 'Contracts: adjustment of long-term economic relations under classical, neoclassical, and relational contract law', *Northwest University Law Review*, 72(6): 854–905. Williamson, O.E. (1979) 'Transaction-cost economics: the governance of contractual relations', *Journal of Law and Economics*, 22(2): 233–261. Desrieux, C., Chong, E. and Saussier, S. (2013) 'Putting all one's eggs in one basket: relational contracts and the management of local public services', *Journal of Economic Behavior and Organization*, 89: 167–186.

relations',[8] more open-ended terms are incorporated into the contract, which then operates more like a framework agreement. These contracts can be long term with the same provider and feature 'a range of processes and techniques used by contract planners to create flexibility in lieu of either leaving gaps or trying to plan rigidly',[9] such as clauses on shared decision making and risk sharing, or rules establishing procedures for resolving conflicts and anticipated challenges informally.[10] The anticipated benefit of relational contracting is that in accepting the inevitable incompleteness of complex outsourcing contracts, it is possible to rely on mutually determined objectives and a collaborative relationship between public and private partners to resolve these uncertainties more effectively (and cheaply) and avoid opportunism. At the same time, where a relational contracting relationship is sufficiently formalized, it carries an implied legal duty of good faith requiring contracting parties to maintain standards trust, cooperation and transparency which can be challenged judicially.[11] The problem is of course that insofar as private

---

[8] Williamson, O.E. (1979) 'Transaction-cost economics: the governance of contractual relations', *Journal of Law and Economics*, 22(2): 233–261, p 238.

[9] Macneil, I.P. (1978) 'Contracts: adjustment of long-term economic relations under classical, neoclassical, and relational contract law', *Northwest University Law Review*, 72(6): 854–905, p 865.

[10] Brown, T.L., Potoski, M., Van Slyke, D.M. (2018) 'Complex Contracting: Management Challenges and Solutions', *Public Administration Review*, 78(5): 661–820. Ball, N. and Gibson, M. (2022) *Partnerships with Principles: Putting Relationships at the Heart of Public Contracts for Better Social Outcomes* [online], Government Outcomes Lab, Blavatnik School of Government and University of Oxford, September, Available from: https://golab.bsg.ox.ac.uk/documents/Partnerships_with_princ iples_final_web.pdf [Accessed 27 February 2024].

[11] *Bates & Others v Post Office Ltd* ((No 3) 'Common Issues') [2019] EWHC 606 (QB) (15 March 2019), para 725, Available from: www.bailii.org/ ew/cases/EWHC/QB/2019/606.html [Accessed 27 February 2024].

providers are treating public contracts opportunistically to extract rent, flexible and relational contracting might be difficult or impossible, and a rather ineffectual governance tool: '[w]hile emphasising trust is explicitly intended to make opportunism and conflict less likely, it also means that if those things do occur, the consequences for one or both parties can be more serious.'[12] In those situations, a more detailed, formalized and transactional contract design might be necessary or inevitable.

Achieving an appropriate balance in contractual drafting between detail and flexibility and between a wider or narrow contracting scope can determine whether an outsourcing relationship is successful or not. As a governance tool, therefore, the public contract may not be perfect but the importance of optimizing its design is central given that in practice, these considerations can be finely balanced. We have seen these issues in the UK, as sectors that introduced outcome-based contracting (where payment for services rendered depends, fully or in part, on the achievement of outcomes specified in the contract but the provider is more or less free to choose how to secure these outcomes) have delivered mixed results.[13] Despite their widespread use in some sectors, there is currently

---

[12] Ball, N. and Gibson, M. (2022) *Partnerships with Principles: Putting Relationships at the Heart of Public Contracts for Better Social Outcomes* [online], Government Outcomes Lab, Blavatnik School of Government and University of Oxford, September, p 21, Available from: https://golab.bsg.ox.ac.uk/documents/Partnerships_with_principles_final_web.pdf [Accessed 27 February 2024].

[13] National Audit Office (2015) *Outcome-Based Payment Schemes: Government's Use of Payment by Results* [online], 15 June, Available from: www.nao.org.uk/wp-content/uploads/2015/06/Outcome-based-paym ent-schemes-governments-use-of-payment-by-results.pdf [Accessed 27 February 2024]. Monitor (undated) *Outcomes-Based Payment: How the Model Works* [online], Available from: https://assets.publishing.serv ice.gov.uk/government/uploads/system/uploads/attachment_data/file/459680/OBP-explainers_sm_v2.pdf [Accessed 27 February 2024]. Social impact bonds, where a social investor finances the contracted

no clear evidence of whether outcomes-based contracts for the delivery of public services have overall been effective at reducing cost and improving innovation.[14] One case study concludes that their flexibility rendered these contracts more resilient and capable of adapting to unpredictable circumstances, such as during the COVID-19 pandemic.[15] Another, however, concludes that providers offer limited

---

services upfront, can be set up to support outcomes-based schemes. See Bridges Fund Management (2019) *Better Outcomes, Better Value: The Evolution of Social Impact Bonds in the UK* [online], March, Available from: www.bridgesfundmanagement.com/wp-content/uploads/2017/08/Bridges-Better-Outcomes-Better-Value-2017-print.pdf [Accessed 27 February 2024]. Savell, L. and Airoldi, M. (2020) 'Outcomes-based contracts in a time of crisis', *Stanford Social Innovation Review* [online], 29 December, Available from: https://ssir.org/articles/entry/outcomes_based_contracts_in_a_time_of_crisis# [Accessed 27 February 2024]. Anastasiu, A. (2023) 'Can social outcomes contracts really catalyse lasting change?', *Oxford Government Outcomes Blog* [online], 10 May, Available from: https://golab.bsg.ox.ac.uk/community/blogs/socs-system-change/ [Accessed 27 February 2024]. Dunbar-Rees, R. (2018) 'Paying for what matters most: the future of outcomes-based payments in healthcare', *Future Healthcare Journal*, 5(2): 98–102. Allcock, C. (2015) 'Outcomes-based commissioning – much promise, but is it something that CCGs can actually deliver on?', *The Health Foundation* [online], 24 September, Available from: www.health.org.uk/blogs/outcomes-based-commissioning-much-promise-but-is-it-something-that-ccgs-can-actually-deliver-on [Accessed 27 February 2024].

[14] ICF International (2015) *Payment by Results: Learning from the Literature* [online], 27 February, Available from: www.nao.org.uk/wp-content/uploads/2015/06/Payment-by-Results-Learning-from-the-Literature.pdf [Accessed 28 February 2024]. National Audit Office (2015) *Outcome-Based Payment Schemes: Government's Use of Payment by Results* [online], 15 June, Available from: www.nao.org.uk/wp-content/uploads/2015/06/Outcome-based-payment-schemes-governments-use-of-payment-by-results.pdf [Accessed 27 February 2024]. Albertson, K. and Fox, C. (2018) *Payment by Results and Social Impact Bonds: Outcome-Based Payment Systems in the UK and US*, Bristol: Policy Press.

[15] Fitzgerald, C., Hameed, T., Rosenbach, F., Macdonald, J.R. and Dixon, J. (2023) 'Resilience in public service partnerships: evidence from the UK Life Chances Fund', *Public Management Review*, 25(4): 787–807.

service intensity in outcomes-based payment schemes in a context of public austerity.[16]

Thus, to optimize the benefit of public contracting, it is important that contracting authorities are well resourced and skilled to draft and manage public contracts effectively so that problems of dependency and the risks of exploitation in incomplete contracts are minimized. 'Contract managers must have the capabilities and information they need to ensure good performance.'[17] This of course means the state must invest in the public sector's capability to manage public contracts (and its long-term relationship with the private sector) effectively – for example, by developing extensive contracting guidance supported by model documentation and a range of training opportunities to ensure public managers have the requisite skills to apply these.[18] To be effective, these must come with

---

[16] Rosenbach, F. and Carter, E. (2020) *Kirklees Integrated Support Service and Better Outcomes Partnership: The First Report from a Longitudinal Evaluation of a Life Chances Fund Impact Bond* [online], Government Outcomes Lab, December, Available from: https://assets.publishing.service.gov.uk/government/uploads/system/uploads/attachment_data/file/1079777/Kirklees_Integrated_Support_Service_and_Better_Outcomes_Partnership_Report.pdf [Accessed 27 February 2024].

[17] Sasse, T., Guerin, B., Nickson, S., O'Brien, M., Pope, T. and Davies, N. (2019) *Government Outsourcing: What Has Worked and What Needs Reform?* [online], September, Institute for Government, p 9, www.instituteforgovernment.org.uk/sites/default/files/publications/government-outsourcing-reform-WEB.pdf [Accessed 27 February 2024].

[18] HM Government (2023) *The Sourcing Playbook* [online], June, Available from: https://assets.publishing.service.gov.uk/media/64901fcc5f7bb700127fac5e/Sourcing_Playbook_Final.pdf [Accessed 26 February 2024]. HM Government (2022) *The Consultancy Playbook* [online], September, Available from: https://assets.publishing.service.gov.uk/media/631f2237e90e077db807dd00/The_Consultancy_Playbook_Version_1.1_September_2022.pdf [Accessed 26 February 2024]. Crown Commercial Service (2021) 'How to write a specification – procurement essentials' [online], 16 November, Available from: www.crowncommercial.gov.uk/news/how-to-write-a-specification-procurement-essentials [Accessed 27 February 2024].

appropriate public resources and incentives for contracting authorities to use them, especially when their aim is to change ineffective contracting behaviour that has become culturally embedded in government departments (for example, risk aversion and short-term outsourcing objectives focused on cheapest price over better quality).[19] It is important that the relevant public decision makers carefully assess the resource implications of these decisions.

Markets

Public outsourcing contracts do not happen in a vacuum but in a context where the state can draw on additional governance tools to adapt and improve the interaction between public and private actors. Given its public authority and spending power, the state can address problems by, for example, threatening to withdraw from the existing outsourcing relationship by re-tendering the services in question when the contract expires or, in some cases, even before. By periodically re-tendering public services, the state can impose accountability on underperforming providers and the possibility of excluding them from participation in future contracts, thereby addressing problems related to both incumbency and exploitation of incomplete contracts. Threatening to change providers in future contracts makes the incompleteness of individual

---

[19]   The Institute for Government, for example, observes that some provisions in the central contracting guidance 'have been routinely ignored, partly because government departments have lacked the capabilities or incentives to implement them. Setting out best practice alone will not be enough to change behaviour and culture that is ingrained' – Sasse, T., Guerin, B., Nickson, S., O'Brien, M., Pope, T. and Davies, N. (2019) *Government Outsourcing: What Has Worked and What Needs Reform?* [online], Institute for Government, p 9, September, www.instituteforgovernment.org.uk/ sites/default/files/publications/government-outsourcing-reform-WEB. pdf [Accessed 27 February 2024].

contracts, and the risk of exploitation, initially less problematic. The private provider cannot just operate strategically but must also maintain its relationship with the public sector beyond the specific contract. The re-tendering process opens up a risk of the provider being replaced as a partner and even cut out of future tenders, so repeat tenderers have a reputational stake in the process. Managers try not to sully the firm's reputation when this might impact on its ability to secure future contracts. By holding contractors to account for past performance, the state may draft contracts more flexibly and relationally, taking some pressure off the contracting instrument as a governance tool as the power of re-tendering can be leveraged to pick up the slack.

The effectiveness of using re-tendering as a governance tool, however, depends on the state's ability to spot both weaknesses in public contracts and exploitative behaviour. It relies on information about contractors' behaviour being transparent and able to be shared and used by different public agencies, for which there has to be capacity within the public administration as well as a suitable regulatory regime. But this is often far from guaranteed. Asymmetries of information, lock-in effects and incumbency advantages affect not only the contract management of existing outsourced structures, but also the re-tendering of public contracts, because at the time of reopening competition for provision of the public service, the public sector will not necessarily have the skills required to extract best value from the market or the ability to neutralize the incumbency advantages of the existing provider through adequate tender design. Considerable resources are necessary to ensure this. It requires that public managers base their decisions on a careful assessment of existing factual evidence – which has to be meticulously collected and assessed – rather than on other considerations such as perception of risk, political convenience or ideology. Besides, the state relies on a public procurement regime that enables it to take account, in the tendering process, of the performance in previous public contracts of potential providers.[20]

Compared to the previous legal regime, the new public procurement legislation has strengthened some important transparency requirements. It requires contracting authorities to publish circumstances where a supplier has breached a contract and this has resulted in full or partial termination, the award of damages or a settlement agreement, or where the contracting authority considers that the supplier is not delivering a public contract to the authority's satisfaction despite being given proper opportunity to improve performance.[21] The purpose of these provisions is to ensure that any contracting issues are made transparent in information that is publicly accessible online and free of charge.[22] Going further, a contracting authority can now exclude a supplier when they have committed a sufficiently serious breach of contract or where they have not performed to the authority's satisfaction despite being given proper opportunity to improve performance.[23] It means that poor performance can, under the new law, be a ground for contracting authorities to exclude a supplier from future procurement processes where the authority considers that it is likely to perform poorly again (taking into account factors such as whether the supplier has taken steps to 'self-clean').[24] In addition, the new law introduces, following their exclusion, the possibility of debarment of individual providers by a minister of state,

---

[20] Crown Commercial Service (2015) *Procurement Policy Note – Taking Account of Suppliers' Past Performance*, Action Note 04/15 [online], 25 March, Available from: https://assets.publishing.service.gov.uk/government/uploads/system/uploads/attachment_data/file/417211/PPN04-15_Supplier_Past_Performance_.pdf [Accessed 27 February 2024].

[21] Section 71 PA2023.

[22] Section 95 PA2023. Transparency is also the purpose of new legal obligations to integrate KPIs into large contracts; see section 52 PA2023.

[23] Schedule 7, para 12 PA2023.

[24] Sections 57 and 58 PA2023.

to avoid public contracts being awarded to unfit suppliers in future.[25]

Other transparency proposals, however, did not make it into the final text of the new legislation. A suggested clause on tax transparency, for example, which would have required contracting authorities to demand the submission of a tax report from multinational suppliers for large contracts, was rejected by the government.[26] Another proposal by the Labour opposition would have strengthened the use of non-performance clawback clauses in public contracts to recover money from underperforming or failing suppliers, but this too was unsuccessful.[27] Nor did the government include proposals to mandate open book accounting in all or some public contracts to introduce greater transparency on providers' profit margins.[28] The current position remains that open book accounting is promoted as best practice in guidelines issued by the Cabinet Office and the National Audit Office, but is currently not universally implemented – clearly in part,

---

[25] The process is set out in sections 59 and 62 PA2023.

[26] Procurement Bill [HL], volume 734, debated on Tuesday 13 June 2023, Deputy Speaker, column 178, Available from: https://hansard.parliam ent.uk/commons/2023-06-13/debates/5F35C5A7-83E8-4E16-A1DF-0E56E4CDF48D/ProcurementBill(Lords) [Accessed 27 February 2024].

[27] Procurement Bill [HL], volume 725, debated on Monday 9 January 2023, Angela Rayner MP, column 353, Available from: https://hansard. parliament.uk/commons/2023-01-09/debates/2936011F-A818-40FC-941B-D53E05672870/ProcurementBill(Lords)#contribution-3E6D9 F2D-79F3-48EA-B595-95CFE45BA872 [Accessed 27 February 2024].

[28] Social Enterprise UK (undated) *House of Commons Public Bill Committee Procurement Bill: Call for Evidence* [online], Available from: https://bills. parliament.uk/publications/49626/documents/2862#:~:text=Howe ver%2C%20the%20Procurement%20Bill%20is,is%20currently%20 not%20universally%20implemented [Accessed 27 February 2024]. O'Brien, A. (undated) 'The Procurement Bill and the future of social value', Social Enterprise UK [online], Available from: www.socialent erprise.org.uk/thought-leadership/the-procurement-bill-and-the-fut ure-of-social-value/ [Accessed 27 February 2024].

at least, for cost reasons.[29] Just as with contracting design, discussed earlier, optimizing the design of public tenders to leverage market competition as a governance tool on existing providers involves a careful balancing exercise. In this, the state weighs the benefits of imposing transparency obligations to ensure accountability against a realistic assessment of the cost and feasibility of policing these obligations and the related risk that commercial providers may be put off participating in tender opportunities by overly strenuous transparency conditions.

In addition to ensuring that poorly performing suppliers are properly held accountable in future tenders, the state can reduce outsourcing problems by minimizing various barriers for smaller suppliers and new entrants bidding for public contracts. The prospect of a diverse pool of new entrants reinforces the state's leverage over existing contractors in re-tendering. Procurement barriers, on the other hand, reduce that leverage, because incumbents can see that they are less likely to lose their privileged position when the contract comes up for re-tender. In this vein, the new public procurement legislation introduces, for the first time in UK public procurement law, a duty for contracting authorities to have regard to the fact that SMEs may face particular barriers to participation and to consider whether such barriers can be removed.[30] In addition, the law introduces several provisions that target specific procedural barriers for SMEs (see the Introduction), foremost among

---

[29] Crown Commercial Service (2015) *Open Book Contract Management Guidance* [online], Available from: https://assets.publishing.service.gov.uk/government/uploads/system/uploads/attachment_data/file/525283/obcm_guidance_final.pdf [Accessed 27 February 2024]. Crown Commercial Service (2016) *Open Book Contract Management*, Information Note 05/16 [online], 24 May, Available from: https://assets.publishing.service.gov.uk/media/5a803a9340f0b62305b89ef9/ppn_open_book_final.pdf [Accessed 27 February 2024].

[30] Sections 12(4) and 86 PA2023.

them the duty for contracting authorities to consider whether the goods or services in question could reasonably be supplied under more than one contract and whether contracts could be split into individual lots.[31] These changes come after over a decade of concerted policy effort to encourage more direct SME participation in public procurement, with outcomes being overall disappointing and still falling well short of central government targets.[32]

These legal provisions are supplemented by various guidance documents and policy notes designed to strengthen

---

[31] Section 18 PA2023. On the previous regime, see Trybus, M. (2018) 'The division of public contracts into lots under Directive 2014/24: minimum harmonisation and impact on SMEs in public procurement?', *European Law Review*, 43(3): 313–342. Herrera Anchustegui, I. (2016) 'Division into lots and demand aggregation – extremes looking for the correct balance?' in G. Skovgaard Ølykke and A. Sanchez-Graells (eds) *Reformation or Deformation of the EU Public Procurement Rules*, Cheltenham: Edward Elgar, pp 125–145.

[32] According to the British Chambers of Commerce, direct SME spending as a proportion of wider public sector procurement spending was only 21 per cent in 2021, far short of the government's target of 33 per cent. See British Chambers of Commerce (2022) 'Only one in five pounds of direct government public procurement spending awarded to SMEs' [online], 12 October, Available from: www.britishchambers.org.uk/news/2022/10/only-one-in-five-pounds-of-direct-government-public-procurement-spending-awarded-to-smes/ [Accessed 27 February 2024]. See the Labour opposition leader's comments at: Procurement Bill [HL], Angela Rayner Excerpts, 2nd reading, 9 January 2023 [online], Available from: www.parallelparliament.co.uk/mp/angela-rayner/deb ate/2023-01-09/commons/commons-chamber/procurement-bill-lords [Accessed 27 February 2024]. The initial consultation on SME access to procurement in 2013 illustrates this as long-standing issue. See HM Government (2013) *Consultation Document: Making Public Sector Procurement More Accessible to SMEs* [online], Available from: https://ass ets.publishing.service.gov.uk/government/uploads/system/uploads/atta chment_data/file/243685/SME_consultation_-_publication_version_-_ 18september.pdf [Accessed 27 February 2024]. For an international perspective, see OECD (2018) *SMEs in Public Procurement: Practices and*

the public sectors' contracting with SMEs, including by improving communication, producing simple and streamlined procurement documentation, adjusting award weighting to incorporate quality and social value and, where possible, ensure that tender opportunities fit the capacity of SMEs, and marking these clearly.[33] A model 'short form' contract for smaller public contracts, designed to help contracting authorities, has been made available to avoid 'the use of overly complex terms which can increase costs and act as a barrier to the involvement of SME'.[34]

Strategies for Shared Benefits [online], 26 October, Available from: www.oecd-ilibrary.org/governance/smes-in-public-procurement_9789264307 476-en?itemId=/content/component/9789264307476-6-en&_csp_= b3bae344869ba595e18d6230c978cd84&itemIGO=oecd&itemContentT ype=chapter [Accessed 27 February 2024].

[33] Crown Commercial Service (2021) 'Crown Commercial Service SME action plan', *Gov.uk* [online], 30 November, Available from: www.gov.uk/government/publications/crown-commercial-service-sme-act ion-plan/crown-commercial-service-sme-action-plan--2 [Accessed 27 February 2024]. Crown Commercial Service (2016) *Procurement Policy Note – Onerous Practices in Procurement and Contracting*, Action Note PPN 10/16 [online], December, Available from: https://assets.publish ing.service.gov.uk/government/uploads/system/uploads/attachment_ data/file/577259/PPN1016-OnerousPracticesinProcurementContract ing__1_.pdf [Accessed 27 February 2024]. Government Commercial Function (2020) *The Social Value Model* [online], December, Available from: https://assets.publishing.service.gov.uk/media/5fc8b7ede90e0 762a0d71365/Social-Value-Model-Edn-1.1-3-Dec-20.pdf [Accessed 26 February 2024]. HM Government (2020) *Procurement Policy Note – Taking Account of Social Value in the Award of Central Government Contracts*, Action Note PPN 06/20 [online], September, Available from: https:// assets.publishing.service.gov.uk/government/uploads/system/uploads/ attachment_data/file/921437/PPN-06_20-Taking-Account-of-Social-Value-in-the-Award-of-Central-Government-Contracts.pdf [Accessed 26 February 2024].

[34] Cabinet Office and Government Legal Department (2022) 'Short form contract', *Gov.uk* [online], updated 1 August 2023, Available from: www.gov.uk/government/collections/short-form-terms-and-con ditions [Accessed 27 February 2024]. See also Cabinet Office (2020) *Procurement Policy Note – Reserving Below Threshold Procurements*, Action

Guidance also expressly encourages authorities to restrict the number of KPIs included in such contracts, to ensure proportionality depending on the value, complexity and criticality of the contract in question, and to desist from imposing overburdensome due diligence requirements that might deter smaller providers.[35] Contracting authorities are further expected, for reasons of transparency and to ensure access, to clearly mark reserved public procurement opportunities for smaller contracts falling below the relevant legal thresholds when publishing the required opportunity notice, and even where a contract is not reserved but considered suitable for SMEs, contracting authorities are expected to mark this clearly.[36]

As with contract design, managing public tenders is a matter of culture and habit as well as resource and skill. For example, where contracting authorities continue to select private providers on the basis of narrow quality criteria and short-term contracting horizons, often prioritizing cheapest price over long term assurances of quality and cost, they can create inefficiencies that materialize at a later date, or increase costs elsewhere in the public sector where private providers reduce their own costs while passing follow-on problems back onto the

Note PPN 11/20 [online], December, p 4, Available from: https://ass ets.publishing.service.gov.uk/media/614c9c0fe90e077a2e2adc44/20210 923-PPN-11_20-Reserving-Below-Threshold-Procurements.docx.pdf [Accessed 26 February 2024].

[35] Cabinet Office (2020) *Procurement Policy Note – Reserving Below Threshold Procurements*, Action Note PPN 11/20 [online], December, p 5, Available from: https://assets.publishing.service.gov.uk/media/614c9c0fe90e077a2 e2adc44/20210923-PPN-11_20-Reserving-Below-Threshold-Procu rements.docx.pdf [Accessed 26 February 2024].

[36] Cabinet Office (2020) *Procurement Policy Note – Reserving Below Threshold Procurements*, Action Note PPN 11/20 [online], December, p 6, Available from: https://assets.publishing.service.gov.uk/media/614c9c0fe90e077a2 e2adc44/20210923-PPN-11_20-Reserving-Below-Threshold-Procu rements.docx.pdf [Accessed 26 February 2024].

state.[37] By prioritizing pricing criteria with narrow governance demands, contracting authorities aiming to drive down public expenditure in the short term tend to signal a preference for partners that are ready to cut expenses, directly or via their supply chains. These are conditions that, often, larger providers and incumbent firms are best placed to satisfy.[38] Contracting authorities may address this problem by giving more weight to quality and social value criteria (further discussed in Chapters One and Seven) in their public procurement, to ensure awards are not made on price alone but instead generate dynamic efficiencies. They may award contracts with a view to creating outcomes relating to the longer term and defined more widely by reference to economic, social and environmental objectives.

But extending contracts to smaller providers does not always reduce problems of exploitation where they too are commercial organizations and can be set up (even as single-shareholder companies) to prioritize value extraction in delivering public contracts, creating the financialized incumbents of tomorrow and perpetuating existing problems of opportunism.[39] For example, Transparency International UK found that the UK

---

[37] Sasse, T., Guerin, B., Nickson, S., O'Brien, M., Pope, T. and Davies, N. (2019) *Government Outsourcing: What Has Worked and What Needs Reform?* [online], Institute for Government, September, p 8, Available from: www.instituteforgovernment.org.uk/sites/default/files/publications/government-outsourcing-reform-WEB.pdf [Accessed 27 February 2024]. Hart, O., Shleifer, A. and Vishny, R. (1997) 'The proper scope of government: theory and an application to prisons', *Quarterly Journal of Economics*, 112(4): 1127–1161, p 1128.

[38] Crown Commercial Service (2023) 'Levelling the playing field: the benefits of working with SMEs and how public sector organisations can make it easier for them to bid for work – procurement essentials' [online], updated 30 August, Available from: www.crowncommercial.gov.uk/news/levelling-the-playing-field-the-benefits-of-working-with-smes-and-how-public-sector-organisations-can-make-it-easier-for-them-to-bid-for-work-procurement-essentials [Accessed 27 February 2024].

[39] For a recent example involving a single-shareholder company, see Mason, R. (2023) 'One of Tories' biggest ever donors profited from

government, in managing the COVID-19 pandemic, awarded £255 million worth of contracts to ten small firms that were at the time less than 60 days old, and considers that this raises 'valid questions as to why these were treated as more qualified for the job, especially given the reported availability of other more established companies'.[40]

Regulation

To address outsourcing problems, the state may choose to combine the contractual governance mechanism with an additional regulatory regime designed to control the contracting relationship, whether by penalizing poor performance or by rewarding good outsourcing behaviour. That layer of regulation may be coupled with the creation of a specialized administrative body or regulatory agency entrusted with its enforcement, although this is not necessary. In the UK, regulatory oversight remains an essential feature in the delivery of many public services, despite advanced outsourcing.[41] Individual regulatory regimes are, however, diverse in terms of their design and scope, and the same type of regulatory power need not always rest with the same authority, even in the same sector. HM Inspectorate of Prisons, for example, is the independent regulatory body that regularly reviews and reports on the conditions and treatment

£135m of NHS contracts', *The Guardian* [online], 20 September, Available from: www.theguardian.com/politics/2023/sep/20/one-of-tories-biggest-ever-donors-frank-hester-profited-from-135m-of-nhs-contracts [Accessed 27 February 2024].

[40] Transparency International UK (2021) *Track and Trace: Identifying Corruption Risks in Public Procurement for the COVID-19 Pandemic* [online], p 23, Available from: www.transparency.org.uk/sites/default/files/pdf/publications/Track%20and%20Trace%20-%20Transparency%20International%20UK.pdf [Accessed 27 February 2024].

[41] Baldwin, R., Cave, M. and Lodge, M. (eds) (2010) *The Oxford Handbook of Regulation*, Oxford: Oxford University Press. Prosser, T. (1999) 'Theorising utility regulation', *Modern Law Review*, 62(2): 196–217.

of people held in Britain's prisons.[42] But while the Inspectorate executes regular reviews, it is HM Prisons and Probation Service, another regulatory agency, that may act on those assessments by way of enforcement where failures are identified.[43]

A common form of regulatory intervention relates to the administration of an ex ante licensing or registration regime. We find these in relation to, for example, privatized utilities and transport services, but also social housing and the social care sector. We do not find them, perhaps surprisingly, for private providers of prison services, which are subject to inspection but not ex ante registration. A particular question relates to the nature and scope of the criteria that a regulatory framework, or a regulatory agency, would design and apply in determining what providers are eligible for registration or licensing, and similarly at what point a provider would be deregistered. These may relate to the provider satisfying economic standards to guarantee the financial viability of their organization; or qualitative criteria relating to aspects of service delivery, including procedures or outcomes. In some cases, these may even include regulatory standards in relation to the competence and conduct of individuals involved in the provision of public services.[44] Different criteria and conditions

---

[42] HM Inspectorate of Prisons (2024) 'Our responsibilities' [online], Available from: www.justiceinspectorates.gov.uk/hmiprisons/about-hmi-prisons/terms-of-reference/ [Accessed 27 February 2024]. Ministry of Justice and the Rt Hon Rory Stewart OBE (2018) 'Written statement to Parliament: prison operator services framework competition', *Gov. uk* [online], 29 November, Available from: www.gov.uk/government/speeches/prison-operator-services-framework-competition [Accessed 27 February 2024].

[43] For concerns raised, see House of Commons Justice Select Committee (2019) 'Oversight of the prison system', in *Prison Governance* [online], 31 October, Available from: https://publications.parliam ent.uk/pa/cm201919/cmselect/cmjust/191/19109.htm [Accessed 27 February 2024].

[44] See, for example, the new powers introduced for the Regulator of Social Housing in the Social Housing (Regulation) Act 2023 in response to

may apply to small providers and large corporate providers (discussed earlier). In the social care sector, for example, the regulatory framework imposes on large care home providers an additional oversight regime, directed by the Care Quality Commission (CQC), which requires them to submit financial information to allow the CQC to assess and monitor their financial sustainability.[45]

Another form of intervention affords regulators the power to regularly inspect and review service providers' performance and make these assessments public. Again, the ambit of these inspections, including their timing and regularity and the publication of inspection outcomes, can vary.[46] Closely related, inspections rely for their effectiveness on being coupled with tangible enforcement procedures to impose accountability on providers where concerns are raised; these procedures may include the imposition of

---

the Grenfell Tower fire tragedy in London: Regulator of Social Housing (2023) *Guidance for New Entrants on Applying for Registration as a Provider of Social Housing* [online], September, Available from: https://assets. publishing.service.gov.uk/government/uploads/system/uploads/atta chment_data/file/1186169/Guidance_new_entrants.pdf [Accessed 27 February 2024]. Trowers & Hamlins (2023) 'Social Housing (Regulation) Act 2023 – essential guide' [online], 23 July, Available from: www.trowers.com/insights/2023/july/social-housing-regulation-act-2023-essential-guide [Accessed 27 February 2024].

[45] Sections 53–57 Care Act 2014, and The Care and Support (Market Oversight Criteria) Regulations 2015. CQC (2022) *Market Oversight of 'Difficult to Replace' Providers of Adult Social Care: Guidance for Providers* [online], May, Available from: www.cqc.org.uk/sites/default/files/2022-05/20220516-market-oversight-guidance-may22-update.pdf [Accessed 27 February 2024].

[46] For example, the CQC may carry out regular comprehensive inspections of care providers but also focused inspections if there is either cause for concern or a change in a care provider's circumstances (such as a corporate takeover, merger or acquisition). See Toersen, N. (2024) 'CQC new inspection framework 2023', *Access* [online], 8 February, Available from: www.theaccessgroup.com/en-gb/blog/hsc-cqc-new-inspection-framework/ [Accessed 27 February 2024].

regulatory sanctions and the administration of complaints procedures. For example, the CQC has certain enforcement powers to take measures against providers that are found to supply poor care standards (involving issues such as high staff absence or poor qualitative delivery). But these powers are notably absent in relation to its monitoring control over large providers' financial viability. Even if it identifies cause for concern that a commercial provider could become financially unstable, it could not intervene to prevent further financial deterioration or even collapse. It could not, for example, require a private company or its investors or directors to take concrete practical action to improve the firm's financial sustainability. In the care home sector, this absence of effective enforcement powers for the CQC has led to the charge of regulation being a blunt tool 'to address one of the commonest causes of poor quality, namely the financial difficulties of the care home owner'.[47]

The state will want to monitor the efficiency and effectiveness of regulatory interventions closely. Given that the point of switching to contractual provision of public services is to improve the delivery of value for money, any inefficiencies (through creating additional cost and complexity) that arise as a result of additional regulatory intervention to govern an outsourcing regime can defeat the point of the outsourcing project.[48] The National Audit Office insists, therefore, that all regulatory bodies 'measure and report performance and outcomes against regulatory objectives, evaluate the real-world

---

[47] Rowland, D. (2019) 'Corporate care home collapse and "light touch" regulation: a repeating cycle of failure', *LSE British Politics and Policy* [online], 8 May, Available from: https://blogs.lse.ac.uk/politicsandpol icy/corporate-care-homes/ [Accessed 26 February 2024].

[48] The National Audit Office costed the annual expenditure of regulators operating in the UK at £4 billion in 2017. See National Audit Office (2017) *A Short Guide to Regulation* [online], September, Available from: www.nao.org.uk/wp-content/uploads/2017/09/A-Short-Guide-to-Regulation.pdf [Accessed 28 February 2024].

impact of interventions, and work in a joined-up way with other organizations in the regulatory landscape'.[49] Regulatory design can be crucial to ensure an efficient allocation of resources. Inspection powers should align with expertise held within the relevant regulatory agency, yet a misalignment can make the process ineffectual. For example, while the CQC may be well equipped to review care quality standards, under the new statutory framework, its competencies are extended to review the financial viability of large corporate providers (although it lacks relevant enforcement powers). These would, arguably, be more effectively placed with a financial regulator.

The worry is not only that inefficiencies in the regulatory oversight of private service providers fail to address outsourcing problems but, further, that a poorly designed regulatory regime will potentially make matters worse. In some cases, ineffectual regulatory responses that precipitate outsourcing failures can be linked to a lack of regulatory independence.[50] In other cases,

---

[49] National Audit Office (2021) *Principles of Effective Regulation* [online], May, p 32, Available from: www.nao.org.uk/wp-content/uploads/2021/05/Principles-of-effective-regulation-SOff-interactive-accessible.pdf [Accessed 28 February 2024].

[50] By way of example, in the privatized water sector it was recently reported that '[t]wo-thirds of England's biggest water companies employ key executives who had previously worked at the watchdog tasked with regulating them' – Ungoed-Thomas, J. (2023) 'Exclusive: UK water giants recruit top staff from regulator Ofwat', *The Guardian* [online], 1 July, Available from: www.theguardian.com/environment/2023/jul/01/exclusive-uk-water-giants-recruit-top-staff-from-regulator-ofwat [Accessed 27 February 2024]. Liberal Democrats (2023) 'Sewage: warnings of "revolving door" between water companies and regulators' [online], 26 June, Available from: www.libdems.org.uk/press/release/sewage-warnings-of-revolving-door-between-water-companies-and-regulators [Accessed 27 February 2024]. But the problem clearly is pervasive across regulated services. According to the UK Committee on Standards in Public Life, in its 2016 cross-sector report on the issues: 'Of the regulators we surveyed, under a third had policies on managing the movement of staff to those they regulate. Even fewer had policies on the recruitment of staff from the organisation or profession they regulate. The Committee

regulatory control creates moral hazard. Returning to social care by way of illustration, strengthened statutory protection was recently afforded, in response to several outsourcing failures, to care home residents in the event of a provider collapse and care home closure; this obliges public authorities to step up to cover temporary costs that residents would otherwise have to pay privately. However, although designed to protect service users, these provisions, according to one commentator, 'introduced a moral hazard into the system: once large care providers knew that the costs of going bust would be picked up by the state there was even less incentive for them to avoid risky behaviour'.[51]

It is theoretically possible for the state to create a layer of regulation that extends public governance elements directly to the oversight and accountability of *all* private providers, and even to couple this with the creation of a specialized administrative body or regulatory agency entrusted with its enforcement. In the UK, however, there are currently no plans to introduce such a broadly scoped regulatory regime. And there are a number of doubts as to the effectiveness of this option. Due to the heterogeneity of economic sectors and activities that would fall under the scope of such a regulatory instrument, regulating the behaviour of all private providers of public services would pose challenges and complexities that outstrip instances of sectoral regulation, and that would

---

is concerned that, where these moves remain unmanaged, regulatory independence is under threat' – Committee on Standards in Public Life (2016) *Striking the Balance: Upholding the Seven Principles of Public Life in Regulation* [online], September, pt 19, Available from: https://assets.pub lishing.service.gov.uk/government/uploads/system/uploads/attachme nt_data/file/554817/Striking_the_Balance__web__-_v3_220916.pdf, [Accessed 27 February 2024].

[51] Rowland, D. (2019) 'Corporate care home collapse and "light touch" regulation: a repeating cycle of failure', *LSE British Politics and Policy* [online], 8 May, Available from: https://blogs.lse.ac.uk/politicsandpol icy/corporate-care-homes/ [Accessed 26 February 2024].

require, presumably, the use of broad and relatively open-ended tools. Such regulatory mechanisms would then need to be of a prudential nature in the sense that, being concerned with the management of risks underpinning the uncertainty involved in long-term contracts, they would take a principles-based approach and be largely geared towards promoting a *culture* of compliance.[52] These mechanisms, therefore, likely result in both ex ante organizational requirements and ex post sanctions for infringements of either the specific requirements or the more general behavioural principles.

Broadly speaking, the intuition here would be that the existence of explicit standards of conduct would guide voluntary behaviour by the actors entrusted with the provision of public services and, otherwise, trigger the adoption of disciplinary measures by the public sector.[53] But just as contracts are incomplete and sometimes relational, the formulation of, for example, a generic code of conduct would likely be premised on at least a comparable (if not higher) level of generality and limited prescriptiveness. This would make it susceptible to multiple interpretations and strategic behaviour as a result of its open texture. This begs the question, then, of whether there is any reason to believe that this additional layer of regulation, facing the same formulation constraints, could deliver better results than identical mechanisms (potentially)

---

[52] Black, J. (2008) 'Forms and paradoxes of principles-based regulation', *Capital Markets Law Journal*, 3(4): 425–457. Van Gestel, N., Koppenjan, J., Schrijver, I., van de Ven, A. and Veeneman, W. (2008) 'Managing public values in public-private networks: a comparative study of innovative public infrastructure projects', *Public Money and Management*, 28(3): 139–145.

[53] For concrete proposals, see the principles proposed for public service providers in a code of conduct in: UNISON (2018) 'UNISON urges government to introduce "code of conduct" for public sector contractors', *Unionweb* [online], 13 February, Available from: http://unionweb.co.uk/unison/unison-urges-government-to-introduce-code-of-conduct-for-public-sector-contractors/ [Accessed 27 February 2024].

specified at contract level. The overarching concern is that a general regulatory regime affecting all private providers, while likely rather costly given its scope, would be far from guaranteeing particularly effective results.

But could a regime be adequately designed to overcome some of these concerns? It is possible to imagine a scenario where a centralized regulatory system – potentially around an 'office of public services' – can be designed to *coordinate* important aspects of managing and overseeing the privatized delivery of public services across different sectors.

On the one hand, this may involve softer coordinating powers, including a form of 'relationship counselling' by setting up fora to mediate conflicts between public and private partners and enable reflection to manage the risk of failing public contracts. It may also involve design of preventative measures. One contribution envisages these softer powers in a 'new agency ... to regulate, share best practice and evaluate outsourcing across Whitehall and the NHS with parallel arrangements for local government and the devolved administrations'.[54] In that regard, an agency may ensure that the state remains forward-looking in managing its resources and resilience. It may collect knowledge of good practice in public outsourcing, by recording past practice, and draw on experience gained across different public actors and sectors to consider how to coordinate activities between them. It might reflect on common structural aspects of good governance aimed at ensuring that transition from one delivery model to another – from privatized to in-house delivery and vice versa – always remains possible and does not become unfeasibly costly.

---

[54] Walker, D. and Tizard, J. (2018) *Out of Contract: Time to Move on from the 'Love In' with Outsourcing and PFI* [online], The Smith Institute, January, p 4, Available from: www.smith-institute.org.uk/wp-cont ent/uploads/2018/01/Out-of-contract-Time-to-move-on-from-the-%E2%80%98love-in%E2%80%99-with-outsourcing-and-PFI.pdf [Accessed 27 February 2024].

This would involve an ongoing assessment of the delivery of public services and their management in order to allow for 'non-crisis' reconsideration of what model better suits the state, given changing circumstances, so that the exercise can be, to some extent, depoliticized. It may also include market engagement activities and encouragement of open book information so that entities that wanted to propose changes in the way public services are run could do that, rather than leaving the initiative solely to the public sector.

On the other hand, there is the possibility of developing specific cross-sector regulatory powers in the hands of a new office or agency with regard to oversight (and a form of reporting and accountability) of supplier organizations, their governance and commitment to delivering public services. The main objective here would be to ensure that organizations continue to operate within the parameters of a public service mission. This could, for example, be modelled on the light touch regulatory regime applied by the current regulator for community interest companies or even on certain aspects of the regulatory function exercised by the Charity Commission.[55] Hutton considers an independent 'office of public services' would be able to oversee a public services reporting regime whereby the non-executive company directors of a public service supplier (he talks of a type of 'public benefit corporation') would 'deliver an independent report to an office of public services each year, giving an account of how the public interest was being achieved'.[56] While this

---

[55] See 'Community interest companies', *Gov.uk* [online], Available from: www.gov.uk/government/organisations/office-of-the-regulator-of-community-interest-companies and 'Charity Commission for England and Wales', *Gov.uk* [online], Available from: www.gov.uk/government/organisations/charity-commission [Accessed 27 February 2024].

[56] Hutton, W. (2018) 'We can undo privatisation. And it won't cost us a penny', *The Guardian* [online], 9 January, Available from: www.theguard ian.com/commentisfree/2018/jan/09/nationalise-rail-gas-water-privat ely-owned [Accessed 27 February 2024].

regime may be applied in specific sectors, it is also possible to imagine a cross-sector framework especially for the delivery of larger and more complex contracts, where the protection against exploitation and failure is crucial.

It would, in essence, extend and strengthen the current transparency obligations that are imposed, in a very light touch manner, on strategic suppliers. Currently, within the Cabinet Office, a Crown representative for strategic suppliers helps manage relationships with them and expects each supplier to provide certain information, through a memorandum of understanding, with a view to improving risk management, efficiencies and accountability.[57] But the current regime is especially limited insofar as there is still no genuine transparency over strategic suppliers' profit margins. For 2021/2022, for example, we know that while the market share of strategic suppliers remained flat, their public sector revenue, mainly from contracts with central government, grew by 24 per cent. In fact, for three of these suppliers, it went up by over 100 per cent, in part as a result of their involvement in the government's response to the COVID-19 pandemic.[58] Because accessing commercial information concerning delivery and profits is difficult or impossible given the rules on commercial secrecy, we can infer but not see exactly how these figures translate

[57] Cabinet Office and Crown Commercial Service (2024) 'Crown representatives and strategic suppliers', *Gov.uk* [online], updated 20 February, Available from: www.gov.uk/government/publications/strategic-suppliers [Accessed 27 February 2024].

[58] Tussell (2022) *UK Strategic Suppliers: 2022 Interim Report* [online], May, Available from: www.tussell.com/hubfs/Tussell%20-%20UK%20Strategic%20Suppliers%202022%20Interim%20Report.pdf?utm_medium=email&_hsmi=212908582&_hsenc=p2ANqtz-_lwWb6YOSthbQHF47pTTap2GYOgsniN-0uE5nTc_-BypdN0YJxcPsG9ETX6YX37fLFEwH5IpuqhBigRbwcjBrAC2nkBg&utm_content=212908582&utm_source=hs_automation [Accessed 26 February 2024].

into profits for these organizations.[59] An office of public services on the other hand could follow up on these figures by holding these suppliers – and other large providers – more fully accountable for ensuring how their operations and governance match up to attaining a public service mission while avoiding extractive behaviour.

While this form of regulation would not be a one-way street (where the state oversees private organizations), but rather involve dialogue between private and public actors, it would potentially deliver important additional accountability over key suppliers, though questions of regulatory effectiveness, and independence, would have to be addressed too.[60] One way of executing this would be through the design of a 'public trust test', much like that recently suggested by Mark Goyder. Goyder first stresses the importance of the 'character' of a public service supplier:

> If only one could have some 'feel' for the character of the company with whom a government department planned to do business, how helpful that would be. Could one identify in advance a company that ... would go the extra mile in a crisis? A company that gave one confidence

---

[59] National Audit Office (2013) *The Role of Major Contractors in the Delivery of Public Services*, presented to the House of Commons on 12 November 2013 [online], p 10, Available from: www.nao.org.uk/wp-content/uplo ads/2013/11/10296-001-BOOK-ES.pdf [Accessed 26 February 2024]. While 'contracts are a matter of public record, it is usually impossible to find out key details like how much profit is built into each one' – Social Enterprise UK (2012) *The Shadow State: A Report about Outsourcing of Public Services* [online], p 12, Available from: www.socialenterprise. org.uk/app/uploads/2022/07/The-Shadow-State-2012.pdf [Accessed 27 February 2024].

[60] See also Witjes, S. and Lozanom, R. (2016) 'Towards a more circular economy: proposing a framework linking sustainable public procurement and sustainable business models', *Resources, Conservation and Recycling*, 112: 37–44.

that it would put its client first, ahead of the temptations of profiteering?

In response to his own question, he proposes a 'trust test' standard providing

both purchasers and sellers with a methodology and a common language for demonstrating and assessing the character of the company and its relational qualities alongside the more transactional aspects. It offers the opportunity for due diligence on the character of a company. The standard also offers simplified processes for smaller organizations.[61]

This could be coupled with, for example, an ongoing reporting system or even a points-based system for companies to ensure they continue to operate in alignment with a public service mission.[62]

---

[61] Goyder, M. (2021) 'Better judgment', *Mark Goyder* [online], 9 August, Available from: http://markgoyder.com/better-judgement/# [Accessed 27 February 2024].

[62] Lonsdale, C., Sanderson, J., Watson, G. and Peng, F. (2016) 'Beyond intentional trust: supplier opportunism and management control mechanisms in public sector procurement and contracting', *Policy & Politics*, 44(2): 289–311.

FOUR

Solutions in Ownership

Public ownership

Problems and associated costs of outsourcing (including its regulation) may lead the public sector to conclude that it would in fact be cheaper and better to bring a public service back under public control. Even just by threatening to take the service in-house, the state can exercise some leverage over existing private contractors. Public sector organizations, therefore, tend to increasingly see the option of bringing services back into public ownership as a strategic governance tool that might improve the delivery of public services and support the long-term development of public capabilities, notwithstanding the broader direction of travel, which has seen a significant rise in outsourcing. Indeed, insourcing happens for a variety of reasons, including in some cases where outsourcing has worked *well*, enabling the public sector, by temporarily handing the service over to the private sector, to improve its capabilities and to eventually reabsorb it into public management.[1]

---

[1] Sasse, T., Nickson, S., Britchfield, C. and Davies, N. (2020) *Government Outsourcing: When and How to Bring Public Services Back into Government Hands* [online], Institute for Government, June, pp 6–7, Available from: www.instituteforgovernment.org.uk/sites/default/files/publicati ons/government-outsourcing-public-services-government-hands.pdf [Accessed 23 February 2024].

Evidence across the UK suggests, however, that re-internalization is currently much more common for services outsourced by local authorities than for centrally outsourced services and that it is often dependent on both sector and context.[2] A relatively rare and therefore important recent example of insourcing in UK central government relates to the decision by the UK Ministry of Justice in 2020 to re-internalize probation services, which had been privatized no earlier than 2015. In announcing the move to insourcing, the Ministry cited the need for greater 'flexibility, control and resilience' as a result of the COVID-19 pandemic, in a sector that suffered from multiple outsourcing failures.[3] On the other hand, growing calls for taking prison services directly back into public hands, for similar reasons, have so far been resisted by government.[4]

---

[2] Sasse, T., Nickson, S., Britchfield, C. and Davies, N. (2020) *Government Outsourcing: When and How to Bring Public Services Back into Government Hands* [online], Institute for Government, June, pp 6 and 16–24, Available from: www.instituteforgovernment.org.uk/sites/default/files/publicati ons/government-outsourcing-public-services-government-hands.pdf [Accessed 23 February 2024]. A recent report for the Welsh Government identified potential for insourcing of currently outsourced services, especially in the areas of facilities management, catering, information and communications technologies, leisure and social care – Welsh Government (2022) *Toolkit for Insourcing in Wales* [online], 19 December, Available from: www.gov.wales/sites/default/files/pdf-versions/2022/ 12/1/1671444331/a-toolkit-for-insourcing-in-wales.pdf [Accessed 27 February 2024].

[3] Grierson, J. (2020) 'Probation services to return to public control after Grayling disasters', *The Guardian* [online], 11 June, Available from: www.theguardian.com/society/2020/jun/11/probation-servi ces-to-return-to-public-control-after-grayling-disasters [Accessed 27 February 2024].

[4] We Own It (undated) 'Prisons work better in public hands' [online], Available from: https://weownit.org.uk/public-ownership/pris ons#:~:text=Who%20owns%20our%20prisons%3F,task%20of%20runn ing%20our%20prisons [Accessed 27 February 2024]. Beard, J. (2023) *The Prison Estate in England and Wales*, House of Commons Library

By taking a service back in-house and under public governance, the state eliminates the risk of exploitation that results from being locked into a public contract that is badly designed, highly formalized and impossible to renegotiate. It can, as a result, also assume greater control over ongoing resource allocation, which it may find helpful – for example, where, in the context of economic austerity, public contract payments are effectively ring-fenced from public budget reductions. In some cases, insourcing may help local governments to generate additional income directly by commercializing certain service elements.[5] By insourcing a service, the state might also find it easier to implement government policy related to either primary service objectives (such as ensuring good access, distribution and quality of service) or a secondary purpose (such as meeting social and environmental standards). It may help, for example, in ensuring consistency of delivery where in-house provision avoids a network of outsourced providers by putting in its place a single (either centralized or decentralized but coordinated) hierarchy. It can be cheaper to bundle different services and identify connections between them, coordinating different public needs, and public agencies may collect information on behalf of the state which other public bodies may use to improve their capacity to deliver other public services. In fact, only the public sector may be capable of addressing false economies that contracting can create where, by saving on the delivery of a specific service by outsourcing it, the state indirectly creates costs elsewhere in the public sector, often as a

Research Briefing [online], 29 June, Available from: https://researchbr iefings.files.parliament.uk/documents/SN05646/SN05646.pdf [Accessed 27 February 2024].

5   Association for Public Service Excellence (2019) *Rebuilding Capacity: The Case for Insourcing Public Services* [online], May, p 23, Available from: https:// meetings.london.gov.uk/documents/s78359/04b%20APSE%20-%20the%20case%20for%20insourcing%20-%20May%202019.pdf [Accessed 27 February 2024].

consequence of the fact that private providers are unconcerned with long-term or distributional issues.[6]

But insourcing bears its own limitations and risks, and decisions to take services back in-house are never cost-free. Once the service operates under public ownership, there is a risk that old problems of politicization, inefficiencies and public debt creep back in. And it is important also to guarantee that switching between public and private delivery, while not cost-free, is a manageable task. Whether it makes sense for the state to withdraw from the outsourcing relationship and move to a public delivery model therefore depends, for one thing, on whether the state retains the administrative capacity to sustain this move. It primarily includes an assessment of whether the state is capable of absorbing the expenditure and demand on its resources that follows from providing multiple public services in-house. Where the state lacks the resources to secure collaborative and commercially acceptable outcomes in outsourced relationships, it can hardly be expected to take on direct provision of the services cheaply or overnight. In particular, in a scenario where public sector capabilities are depleted after a period of privatization and economic austerity, a strategy of re-internalization requires significant investment and adequate change management. For the state to successfully insource after a period of outsourcing, it must therefore keep enough capacity within the public sector to be able to withdraw from the outsourcing relationship. This means keeping open the possibility of transition by retaining a minimum of resources and information, to avoid making private delivery self-perpetuating by creating path dependencies (discussed in Chapters Two and Three).

---

[6] Andersson, F., Jordahl, H. and Josephson, J. (2019) 'Outsourcing public services: contractibility, cost, and quality', *CESifo Economic Studies*, 65(4): 349–372.

In practice, the state would first have to invest in public management capabilities to support in-house delivery and then assess whether this investment will be amortized by resulting cost savings. There is no reason in principle to assume that the amount required necessarily outstrips what the state might otherwise have to invest in outsourcing public services to the private sector. This, after all, remains an empirical question that should take into account, inter alia, the risks of substandard private delivery and associated cost. The state, however, has to assess carefully whether the improvements it expects to derive from the direct public provision of the service exceed the cost of switching governance and delivery model. The Institute for Government cautions that

> while insourcing services may offer government bodies benefits, these should not be overstated. The private sector will continue to have expertise, capability and a capacity for innovation that government does not. And while many believe greater insourcing will deliver large cost savings, there is limited robust evidence to support this, and some expect the costs of insourced services to rise over time.[7]

Insourcing does not avoid the difficulties of defining and measuring many qualitative aspects of complex public services – which remain equally important (and elusive) in the direct relationship between the public sector provider and service users (be they citizens or another branch of the

---

[7]   Sasse, T., Nickson, S., Britchfield, C. and Davies, N. (2020) *Government Outsourcing: When and How to Bring Public Services Back into Government Hands* [online], Institute for Government, June, p 7, Available from: www. instituteforgovernment.org.uk/sites/default/files/publications/gov ernment-outsourcing-public-services-government-hands.pdf [Accessed 23 February 2024].

public sector).[8] If it is difficult to establish the extent to which outsourced provision would meet hard-to-measure qualitative aspects of a public service (for example, an appropriate level of interpersonal care), it is no less difficult to forecast potential delivery issues on those same aspects in relation to public provision. This analysis is affected by the same uncertainties that make the design of outsourcing contracts difficult or expensive to draft. However, in-house delivery does change the governance focus related to these risks and uncertainties, and places them strictly under a public governance umbrella. It is important, therefore, to support these decisions by strong operative logics and credible and viable plans to ensure that in-house delivery will be both cheaper and better than outsourcing. This may require case-by-case qualitative analysis and involve risk and uncertainty in both directions. Finding a uniform methodology or model to ensure those outcomes is unlikely and, given some of the concerns, insourcing is unlikely to be a wholesale solution to public outsourcing problems but, rather, dependent on context. Timing too can be crucial. For example, the early termination of an outsourcing contract, if disputed, can lead to litigation and potentially to an award of monetary compensation to the incumbent private provider.[9] These decisions therefore may be effectively time-limited to windows of opportunity around the expiry of outsourcing contracts or other arrangements. On the other hand, where outsourcing providers are in breach of their own public

---

[8] For discussion of the external quality dimension of public service delivery, see Osborne, S.P., Radnor, Z., Kinder, T. and Vidal, I. (2015) 'The SERVICE framework: a public-service-dominant approach to sustainable public services', *British Journal of Management*, 26(3): 424–438.

[9] HM Treasury (2015) *PPP Policy Note: Early Termination of Contracts* [online], June, Available from: https://assets.publishing.service.gov.uk/media/5a80c69fed915d74e33fc567/PPP_terminations_policy_note.pdf [Accessed 27 February 2024].

contract, the state may find it has no other realistic option than to step in.

An important aspect in insourcing decisions is identifying the most appropriate public ownership design, because lack of a suitable design might drive up costs or reduce service quality. There is no single form of insourcing – it is important to select the right institutional and legal 'fit'. The state may choose to retake the service fully in-house or set up an organization to deliver the service, such as a wholly or jointly owned company, over which the public sector exercises control, or it might set up a public–private partnership for delivery.[10] Likewise, a contracting authority may take back the service itself or incorporate the service into another department, or it may collaborate with other public agencies to create a better and more integrated service structure.[11] Alternatively, it might even consider acquiring a 'golden share' in a supplier company to strengthen public control but not give direct powers to political officials, which would risk politicization of its management.[12]

[10] Sasse, T., Nickson, S., Britchfield, C. and Davies, N. (2020) *Government Outsourcing: When and How to Bring Public Services Back into Government Hands* [online], Institute for Government, June, p 13, Available from: www.instituteforgovernment.org.uk/sites/default/files/publications/government-outsourcing-public-services-government-hands.pdf [Accessed 23 February 2024]. Certain conditions will determine whether 'vertical' or 'horizontal' arrangements would be excluded from the public procurement regime under Schedule 2, paras 2 and 3 PA2023 (codifying the 'Teckal' and 'Hamburg' exemptions), as per clause 5 of the draft Procurement Act 2023 (Miscellaneous Provisions) Regulations 2024, Available from: https://assets.publishing.service.gov.uk/government/uploads/system/uploads/attachment_data/file/1163167/230615_DRAFT_Procurement_Act_2023__Miscellaneous_Provisions__Regulations_2024_-_consultation_version.pdf [Accessed 23 February 2024].

[11] Sullivan, H. and Skelcher, C. (2002) *Working Across Boundaries: Collaboration in Public Services*, Berlin: Springer.

[12] Hogan Lovells (2015) *Going for Gold: How Golden Shares Can Help Lock In Mission for Social Enterprises*, Report prepared for Big Society Capital

Where outsourcing is reversed, there is no strong rationale for a systematic rule to either transition back to whichever public ownership form preceded privatization of the service or impose a one-size-fits-all model.[13] Again, decisions have to be adopted on a case-by-case basis and in a manner which ensures that the chosen public ownership form is apt to overcome or minimize the shortcomings of privatized forms of outsourced delivery.

Regardless of where an individual decision falls, the main consideration should be the identification of a public ownership form that addresses the particular issue(s) that made the outsourcing arrangement inoperative or defective. The source and type of non-contractible and/or idiosyncratic elements of the service and its management should be taken into account. If the main issue derives from the difficulty in anticipating changes in service needs or technological developments, it could well be that all forms of public ownership are largely interchangeable. However, if the main issue derives from the need to be able to impose government policy, it could well be that forms that do not involve arm's-length management (for example, a public agency or government department) are better suited than those that do (for example, separate corporate entities). It may also be that the main dysfunction of the outsourced arrangement derives from the inability to take into account the needs of specific classes of stakeholder and to facilitate co-design or co-production of the public services in a way that is not captured by the self-interest of the private provider, in which case the design of public ownership may lead to solutions very close to those discussed in Chapter Five, on sustainable ownership. Reflecting on this,

---

[online], pp 7–9 and 19–20, Available from: www.hoganlovells.com/~/media/hogan-lovells/pdf/publication/4878744v1golden-share-report-final-formlwdlib01_pdf.pdf [Accessed 27 February 2024].

[13] Here, the standard criteria for a decision between public and private ownership do not apply. See Shleifer, A. (1998) 'State versus private ownership', *Journal of Economic Perspectives*, 12(4): 133–150.

the Welsh Government's analysis of insourcing in relation to social care, as an example, concludes: 'There is a compelling case to minimise the presence of extractive providers in local care markets. However, wholescale insourcing could undermine the valuable contribution of the third sector and democratically owned provision, which provides enhanced reach and reciprocity in communities and underpins the foundational economy approach.'[14]

Insourcing decisions should result in an efficient decision-making hierarchy, allocating discretion (see Chapter One) to those public agents best placed to secure non-contractible elements of the public service in question; this would ensure that the process of bargaining that kept the contractual governance of the outsourced public service exposed to risks of exploitation is effectively reversed and replaced. What institutional form is best suited to achieve this will need to be decided on a case-by-case basis.

Thus, rather than seeing insourcing as a tool to fully re-internalize services, it is best seen as a strategic and flexible mechanism for the state to assume various levels and forms of control. One commentator has proposed the form of a public 'foundation share in each privatised utility as a condition of its licence to operate, requiring the utility to reincorporate as a public-benefit company', affording government 'the right to appoint independent non-executive directors whose role would be see that the public interest purposes of the [public-benefit company] were being discharged as promised'.[15] The public services union Unison, on the other hand, has made proposals

[14] Welsh Government (2022) *A Toolkit for Insourcing in Wales* [online], 19 December, Available from: www.gov.wales/sites/default/files/pdf-versions/2022/12/1/1671444331/a-toolkit-for-insourcing-in-wales.pdf [Accessed 27 February 2024].

[15] Hutton, W. (2018) 'We can undo privatisation. And it won't cost us a penny', *The Guardian* [online], 9 January, Available from: www.theguard ian.com/commentisfree/2018/jan/09/nationalise-rail-gas-water-privat ely-owned [Accessed 27 February 2024].

for mutual and democratic forms of public ownership, seeing 'no real reason why mutual approaches cannot be implemented within the public sector'.[16] Clearly, there is room for the state to experiment with a spectrum of public ownership designs.

Private ownership

Aside from considering the different options for public ownership, the state may turn to experimentation in *private* (corporate) ownership design in order to improve public contracting: it may choose to carefully select certain types of private partner in accordance with defined ownership criteria, accepting only those criteria which are deemed suitable for an organization providing public services.[17] Doing so, it effectively co-opts the private supplier's ownership design into the outsourcing model as an additional governance safeguard, supplementing the contractual mechanism. By ensuring that the objectives of the private partner aligns more closely with the state's public governance objectives, the intention is to minimize (though not fully avoid) the risk that incomplete contracts and dependency will be exploited.[18] Where gaps and ambiguities exist in public contracts, the provider organization

---

[16] UNISON (2013) *Mutual Benefit? Should Mutuals, Co-Operatives and Social Enterprises Deliver Public Services?* [online], p 30, Available from: www.unison.org.uk/content/uploads/2013/06/On-line-Catalogue199463.pdf [Accessed 27 February 2024].

[17] Boeger, N. (2018) 'Public procurement and business for value: looking for alignment in law and practice', in A. Sanchez-Graells (ed) *Smart Public Procurement and Labour Standards: Pushing the Discussion after RegioPost*, Oxford: Hart Publishing, pp 115–139. Barraket, J., Keast, R. and Furneaux, C. (2015) *Social Procurement and New Public Governance*, Abingdon: Routledge.

[18] Besley, T. and Ghatak, M. (2003) *Incentives, Choice and Accountability in the Provision of Public Services*, ESRC Centre for Analysis of Risk and Regulation Discussion Paper No 14, Available from: http://eprints.lse.ac.uk/36001/1/Disspaper14.pdf [Accessed 27 February 2024].

is expected to fill and resolve them in a way that the state itself would have done had it anticipated the gap or ambiguity at the time it drafted the contract. This reduces the potential for conflict in the contracting relationship, because key aspects of public and private governance are more aligned, creating more room for trust between the contracting partners and potentially avoiding formalization in overly detailed public contracts. With the provider committed to these ownership criteria, the contracting authority may ultimately be more confident to experiment in relational contract design, accommodating greater flexibility and less prescription as well as a more iterative form of service delivery for details that are difficult to pre-specify. It may be prepared to simplify and formulate public contracts in a more open-ended way with more confidence that conflicts can be resolved informally, avoiding costly formalization or disputes. The contracting partners might even eventually establish better long-term relationships based on mutual collaboration, because the contracting authority can be more confident that the provider's governance incentives align with its own.[19]

There are overlaps with the corporate models we might find in a strategic public ownership design. In taking a service back under public control, the state might also choose a particular ownership design to exercise direct control over the provider

[19] Hall, K., Miller, R. and Millar, R. (2016) 'Public, private or neither? Analysing the publicness of health care social enterprises', *Public Management Review*, 18(4): 539–557. Frith, L. (2014) 'Social enterprises, health-care provision and ethical capital', *Social Enterprise Journal*, 10(2): 105–120. Millar, R., Hall, K. and Miller, R. (2016) *Increasing the Role of Social Business Models in Health and Social Care: An Evidence Review* [online], Public Policy Institute for Wales, January, Available from: www.wcpp.org.uk/wp-content/uploads/2019/02/PPIW-Report-The-role-of-SBMs-in-health-and-social-care-REVISED.pdf [Accessed 27 February 2024]. Brown, L.K. and Troutt, E. (2004) 'Funding relations between nonprofits and government: a positive example', *Nonprofit and Voluntary Sector Quarterly*, 33(1): 5–27.

(for example, via a fully or majority state-owned company, or by taking a public golden share, discussed earlier). In contrast to public ownership, however, this solution maintains a contractual mechanism of control as a central element of both governance and delivery, but complemented by conditions that ensure the private ownership design steers the provider and public authority in the same direction.

The reference to corporate *ownership* in this context, as a matter linked closely to its governance, relates to a bundle of rights in the private corporate organization that will typically be set out in its constitution or, by default, in the relevant law on business organizations. These are *not* what in legal terms render someone an 'owner' of the company (in legal terms, corporate organizations are not assets that can be owned – as separate legal persons, they 'own' themselves). Yet, in practical terms, holders of these rights are in a position to exercise important elements of ownership in the organization. Those holding beneficiary rights can expect their own interests to be prioritized by the corporation's decision-makers. Typically, these rights are set out in the rules on corporate purpose and the fiduciary duties of directors. Control rights, on the other hand, relate to the allocation of key decision-making power within the organization, the exercise of which may be direct or, through rights to appoint and to dismiss, and to hold those running the organization to account, indirect. Economic rights in turn determine how and to whom profits (and assets) may be distributed or indeed what limits are placed on the distribution of profits. These three elements, taken together, determine key parameters of how the organization is governed: its purpose, who has power to control decisions and what happens to profit.

In UK company law, in the default version of the company limited by shares, these rights currently prioritize shareholders. Company directors are responsible for controlling the company day-to-day but they must in law run the company for the benefit of their shareholders, even when having 'regard' for the concerns of other stakeholders, such as consumers, employees and wider society (as discussed further in Chapter Two). Shareholders hold important governance rights of intervention, notably the right to appoint and dismiss company directors and to hold the corporate board to account for their decisions. Equivalent rights do not currently exist for other stakeholders in the firm. Shareholders (but not stakeholders) may also expect to receive a share in the company's profit, either by distribution as dividend (at the directors' discretion) or indirectly through the appreciation of their shares in the company. These priorities are reflected by default in the company legal and governance framework, although they may be altered and tailored by individual companies in drafting their own corporate articles of association.

By prioritizing shareholders in this way, the UK company legal form has the advantage of making itself attractive to equity investors. From the state's point of view, however, the company has a potential governance problem built into its design – its focus on capital accumulation, which renders it attractive for commercial purposes, is precisely what in the public contracting relationship can augment problems of value extraction by creating the possibility for equity investors and directors collaboratively (and incentivized by performance-linked executive remuneration) to prioritize short-term financial objectives and run it simply to extract profit as rent.[20] While there is nothing in UK company law to mandate that directors prioritize short-term investment returns (in fact, by asking directors to consider the interests of stakeholders, the law encourages an inclusive perspective in the pursuit of shareholder value), when companies do choose to prioritize value extraction for their shareholders, there is currently little in the

[20] Christophers, B. (2020) *Rentier Capitalism: Who Owns the Economy and Who Pays for It?* London: Verso. Ireland, P. (1999) 'Company law and the myth of shareholder ownership', *The Modern Law Review*, 62(1): 32–57.

UK's default legal provisions that prevents them from doing so. Coupled with a permissive wider regulatory environment and corporate governance framework (see further Chapter Two), this legal design can act as enabler of a financialized corporate governance model. But in a public outsourcing context, financialized corporate governance has the concrete effect of widely misaligning the incentives of public and private partners (again, see the discussion in Chapter Two) – of widening the 'governance gap' the state has to bridge to manage the outsourcing relationship and exacerbating existing risks of exploitation of contractual incompleteness and incumbency.

Given existing flexibilities in company law that allow for contractual corporate design, and in the law of business organizations more generally, a range of variations of corporate ownership exist or can be configured in which key governance elements relating to purpose, power and profit are less, or not at all, investor centred. Growing interest in these variations of corporate ownership links directly to the wider current debate over how corporations may in future contribute to a more sustainable version of our existing capitalist economies.[21] Concretely, it is about generating financially self-sustaining firms that create sustainable economic value – by legal design, to prevent or temper financialized forms of corporate governance that are extractive (see further Chapters Five and Six).

---

[21] Sjåfjell, B. and Richardson, B.J. (eds) (2015) *Company Law and Sustainability: Legal Barriers and Opportunities*, Cambridge: Cambridge University Press. Kelly, M. (2012) *Owning Our Future: The Emerging Ownership Revolution*, Oakland, CA: Berrett-Koehler. Boeger, N. (2020) 'Sustainable corporate governance: trimming or sowing?', in M. Pieraccini and T. Novitz (eds) *Legal Perspectives on Sustainability*, Bristol: Policy Press, pp 101–123. Kavadis, N. and Thomsen, S. (2023) 'Sustainable corporate governance: a review of research on long-term corporate ownership and sustainability', *Corporate Governance: An International Review*, 31(1): 198–226. Villalonga, B. (2018) 'The impact

Instead, corporate ownership here intends to support a corporate governance model concerned with economic, social and environmental aspects of sustainability, generating wealth and prosperity, not simply profit.[22] This is based on the understanding that in economies which are expected to produce welfare for their societies, the opportunity to derive profit should only ever be seen as an incentive for firms (even those that are 'for profit') to create value that benefits society, not as an end in itself – even more so when these firms are supplying public services on behalf of the state.[23] Sustainability and social value, as it is applied in the UK public procurement context and related to long-term social, economic and environmental objectives (see Chapters One and Seven), can be used interchangeably in describing this key idea.[24]

Sustainable corporate ownership can be configured in various ways (see further Chapter Five). Beneficiary rights may no longer rest with financial investors exclusively or as a matter of priority. Instead, the organization would be committed to a purpose prioritizing factors other than the benefit of its shareholders. The firm may choose to hold its directors accountable for balancing the interests of their shareholders against those of their wider stakeholders, including the environment and society stakeholders. Likewise, shareholders may no longer retain the exclusive governance right to hold the corporate board to account for running

of ownership on building sustainable and responsible businesses', *Journal of the British Academy*, 6(s1): 375–403.

[22] Kelly, M. and Howard, T. (2019) *The Making of a Democratic Economy: How to Build Prosperity for the Many*, Oakland, CA: Berrett Koehler.

[23] Boeger, N. (2021) *Amending UK Company Law for a Regenerative Economy* [online], Institute of Directors, Available from: https://betterbusinessact. org/wp-content/uploads/2021/05/IoD-CG-Centre-Amending-UK-Company-Law.pdf [Accessed 27 February 2024].

[24] Social Enterprise UK (2023) *The Social Value Roadmap 2032* [online], June, Available from: www.socialenterprise.org.uk/seuk-report/the-soc ial-value-roadmap/ [Accessed 11 March 2024].

the firm, a right which ensures strategic decisions reflect the investors' own interests. Instead, a sustainable corporate design might open governance rights – including power to impose accountability but also to take decisions directly – to other corporate stakeholders, including employees and consumers. Finally, economic rights affording shareholders the benefit of a share in the company's profit may be replaced by either an alternative distribution mechanism (for example, distribution to employee or community members) or a restraint or even prohibition on profit distribution to ensure they are invested in the pursuit of purpose.

In public service outsourcing, if the selection of financialized private providers exacerbates risks of exploitation because incentives of private and public partners are widely misaligned, then by selecting providers in sustainable corporate ownership, contracting authorities may reverse that very dynamic. They may achieve a closer alignment of incentives between public and private outsourcing partners, narrowing the governance gap the state has to bridge to successfully manage the contracting relationship and thus reducing the risk of outsourcing failure. Sustainable forms of corporate ownership are, in this way, co-opted into the governance of the outsourcing contract. Contracting authorities in the UK currently make only limited use of this solution, however, with two exceptions.

First, the new public procurement legislation continues, as under the previous regulations, to permit contracting authorities to reserve the award of certain public contracts under a 'light touch' regime to mutual organizations, set up to deliver a public service, that are owned by their employees (so-called 'public service mutuals').[25] The thrust of this regime

---

[25] Section 33 PA2023, and see the analogous regime for supported employment providers in section 32 PA2023. See also the draft Procurement Act 2023 (Miscellaneous Provisions) Regulations 2024,

is that the governance of a public service mutual creates advantages in the delivery of public contracts that justify a reserved award procedure in relation to certain, mainly person-centred, services that fall within the light touch legal regime. However, the regime represents an exception to the general prohibition under public procurement law of limiting access to procurement contracts to any type of provider. Unlike in other countries, the UK does not have a more systemic preference for non-profit providers – for example, by constitutionally protecting their role in certain sectors, such as social and health care.[26] In fact, a proposed clause in the 2022–2023 Procurement Bill that suggested such a provision, was rejected in parliamentary debate.[27]

Second, the UK government pursues a softer policy to support the award of public contracts to deliver mainly people-centred services in sectors like health, social care and education, where service needs are more complex and interpersonal, to VCSE organizations.[28] The government describes VCSE

Available from: https://assets.publishing.service.gov.uk/government/uplo ads/system/uploads/attachment_data/file/1163167/230615_DRAFT_ Procurement_Act_2023__Miscellaneous_Provisions__Regulations_20 24_-_consultation_version.pdf [Accessed 23 February 2024].

[26] For discussion, see the contributions in the special issue on the *Spezzino* case law in *European Procurement & Public Private Partnership Law Review* (2016) 11(1).

[27] It would have introduced a requirement for non-profit organizations to be considered alongside for-profit providers for awards of light touch services which tend to be person centred, with a plan in the long term to 'get rid of all financialised provision and see it all in non-profit hands' – Procurement Bill [HL], volume 823, debated on Monday 11 July 2022, Baroness Bennet of Manor Castle, column 342GC, Available from: https://hans ard.parliament.uk/lords/2022-07-11/debates/B1AC0045-EDC1-4A84-B6BC-4B301BB673C2/ProcurementBill(HL) [Accessed 13 April 2024]. However, that plan did not attract a parliamentary majority to pass.

[28] Tussell (2021) *UK Public Procurement through VCSEs, 2016–2020*, Report for the Department for Culture, Media and Sport [online], Available

organizations as 'the wide range of organisations that exist **with a social or environmental purpose**'[29] or 'any organisation (incorporated or not) working with a social purpose', typically referring to organizations operating as part of the third sector or social economy.[30] The practical support afforded to VCSE organizations aligns in many ways with initiatives designed to create better access to public procurement opportunities for commercial SMEs (discussed in Chapter Three). This makes sense insofar as smaller VCSE organizations will be looking for support measures similar to those extended to SMEs – from simplification and adjustment of contract sizes through to stronger market engagement and transparency, as well as the availability of a reserved procedure for smaller contracts that fall below a legally defined threshold (below-threshold contracts – discussed in Chapter Seven). The government's VCSE policy encourages all of these.[31] In addition, contracting authorities are encouraged to mark even non-reserved tender opportunities that are suitable for VCSE suppliers, indicating

from: https://assets.publishing.service.gov.uk/government/uploads/sys tem/uploads/attachment_data/file/1069635/UK_Public_Sector_Procur ement_through_VCSEs.pdf [Accessed 27 February 2024]. See Rees, J. (2014) 'Public sector commissioning and the third sector: old wine in new bottles?', *Public Policy and Administration*, 29(1): 45–63.

[29] Department for Digital, Culture, Media, and Sport (2022) *The Role of Voluntary, Community, and Social Enterprise (VCSE) Organisations in Public Procurement* [online], August, p 8 [emphasis in original], Available from: https://assets.publishing.service.gov.uk/government/uploads/sys tem/uploads/attachment_data/file/1100749/The_role_of_Voluntary_ _Community__and_Social_Enterprises_in_public_procurement.pdf [Accessed 27 February 2024].

[30] Cabinet Office (2021) *A Guide to Reserving Below Threshold Procurements* [online], p 2, Available from: https://assets.publishing.service.gov.uk/ government/uploads/system/uploads/attachment_data/file/1014494/ 20210818-A-Guide-to-Reserving-Below-Threshold-Procurements.pdf [Accessed 27 February 2024].

[31] Department for Culture, Media and Sport (2023) 'DCMS action plan to engage the voluntary, community and social enterprise sectors in its

to the latter that their bids will be welcome and supported – although a marker alone does not mean contracts are eventually awarded to VCSE organizations.[32] In practice, however, as with SMEs, outcomes continue to fall short of the aspirations set for these policies, even after several years.[33] Overall, VCSE organizations are still only awarded a small minority of public contracts delivering mainly localized person-centred services, and within that share, a few larger charities still dominate the sector's access to government contracts.[34] The majority of opportunities for VCSE organizations arise

supply chain', *Gov.uk* [online], 30 March, Available from: www.gov.uk/government/publications/dcms-action-plan-to-engage-the-voluntary-community-and-social-enterprise-sectors-in-its-supply-chain/dcms-action-plan-to-engage-the-voluntary-community-and-social-enterprise-sectors-in-its-supply-chain#appendix-a-useful-links [Accessed 27 February 2024].

[32] Department for Digital, Culture, Media, and Sport (2022) *The Role of Voluntary, Community, and Social Enterprise (VCSE) Organisations in Public Procurement* [online], August, p 30 et seq, Available from: https://assets.publishing.service.gov.uk/government/uploads/system/uploads/attachment_data/file/1100749/The_role_of_Voluntary__Community__and_Social_Enterprises_in_public_procurement.pdf [Accessed 27 February 2024].

[33] HM Government (2011) *Open Public Services White Paper* [online], 1 July, Available from: https://assets.publishing.service.gov.uk/media/5a7cd5bb40f0b65b3de0b746/OpenPublicServices-WhitePaper.pdf [Accessed 27 February 2024].

[34] Department for Digital, Culture, Media, and Sport (2022) *The Role of Voluntary, Community, and Social Enterprise (VCSE) Organisations in Public Procurement* [online], August, p 4, Available from: https://assets.publishing.service.gov.uk/government/uploads/system/uploads/attachment_data/file/1100749/The_role_of_Voluntary__Community__and_Social_Enterprises_in_public_procurement.pdf [Accessed 27 February 2024]. See also Tussell (2018) 'New research shows slow growth on awards to social enterprises' [online], 23 July, Available from: www.tussell.com/insights/tussell-social-enterprise-uk-research-shows-slow-growth-on-awards-to-community-interest-companies-cics [Accessed 27 February 2024]. Tussell (2021) *UK Public Procurement through VCSEs, 2016–2020*, Report for the Department for Culture, Media and Sport [online], Available

with local authorities, much less with central government.[35] Responsibility for government policies on procuring from VCSE organisations does not rest with the Cabinet Office or the Crown Commercial Service, as for other initiatives, but rather with the VSCE Crown Representative, a role created within the Department for Culture, Media and Sport. The government's VCSE strategy remains, looking at the distribution of resources and responsibilities, a policy separate and distinct from other, mainstream, central procurement policies. At present, relatively few policy initiatives at central government level are specifically aimed at the VSCE sector.[36]

---

from: https://assets.publishing.service.gov.uk/media/625ecdd7d3bf7 f600d4056a4/UK_Public_Sector_Procurement_through_VCSEs.pdf [Accessed 27 February 2024].

[35] Department for Digital, Culture, Media, and Sport (2022) *The Role of Voluntary, Community, and Social Enterprise (VCSE) Organisations in Public Procurement* [online], August, pp 30 et seq, Available from: https://ass ets.publishing.service.gov.uk/government/uploads/system/uploads/atta chment_data/file/1100749/The_role_of_Voluntary__Community_ _and_Social_Enterprises_in_public_procurement.pdf [Accessed 27 February 2024].

[36] Recently among them, a (rather short) guidance document and action plan on securing better access to public procurement opportunities for VSCE and a (longer) report: Cabinet Office, Department for Culture, Media and Sport, and Department for Digital, Culture, Media and Sport (2021) 'VCSE: a guide to working with government', *Gov.uk* [online], updated 25 October 2023, Available from: www.gov.uk/guidance/vcses-a-guide-to-working-with-government [Accessed 27 February 2024]; Department for Culture, Media and Sport (2023) 'DCMS action plan to engage the voluntary, community and social enterprise sectors in its supply chain', *Gov.uk* [online], 30 March, Available from: www.gov. uk/government/publications/dcms-action-plan-to-engage-the-volunt ary-community-and-social-enterprise-sectors-in-its-supply-chain/ dcms-action-plan-to-engage-the-voluntary-community-and-social-ent erprise-sectors-in-its-supply-chain#appendix-a-useful-links [Accessed 27 February 2024]; Department for Digital, Culture, Media, and Sport (2022) *The Role of Voluntary, Community, and Social Enterprise (VCSE) Organisations in Public Procurement* [online], August, pp 30 et seq, Available

More fundamentally, the design of these policies and their rather formulaic framing, centred on the VCSE moniker and narrowly defined public service mutuals, does little to explicitly develop opportunities of incorporating sustainable corporate ownership design more widely into public outsourcing to improve the governance of public contracting. The government might consider extending these policies to create more room for experimentation in the selection of providers in sustainable ownership. VCSE organizations – charities, social enterprises, community businesses, cooperatives and so on – operate as various forms of sustainable corporate ownership, but some other corporate forms in the wider economy now do so too (see further Chapter Five). The focus on 'social purpose' in the VCSE definition oversimplifies and narrows what in reality are highly diverse sustainable corporate designs, the range of which is currently growing and developing at speed. Nor is sustainable design limited to smaller or even medium-sized companies (consider, for example, foundation-owned firms – see the recent move towards foundation ownership by Patagonia, a multinational, referred to in Chapter Five). A great deal of variation and experimentation is possible and available.

The state, given its political responsibility but limited administrative capacity to provide public services directly, may therefore usefully recentre its current public procurement policies by moving beyond VCSE organizations and incorporating a spectrum of sustainable corporate design

---

from: https://assets.publishing.service.gov.uk/government/uploads/sys tem/uploads/attachment_data/file/1100749/The_role_of_Voluntary_ _Community__and_Social_Enterprises_in_public_procurement.pdf [Accessed 27 February 2024]. See also Tussell (2021) *UK Public Procurement through VCSEs 2016–2020*, Report for the Department for Culture, Media and Sport [online], Available from: https://assets.publishing.serv ice.gov.uk/media/625ecdd7d3bf7f600d4056a4/UK_Public_Sector_Pr ocurement_through_VCSEs.pdf [Accessed 27 February 2024].

more fully into attempts to co-opt the ownership design of private organizations into the delivery of public welfare. It may reframe these policies expressly to prioritize the selection, in certain circumstances, of sustainable forms of private corporate ownership in public service outsourcing, based on the criteria of corporate purpose, decision-making power and profit distribution. By centring on these criteria for providers in sustainable ownership, the state has the opportunity of creating, through public procurement, the experimental dynamic of a competitive 'race to the top' where providers offering a more (or more adequate) sustainable corporate design might fare better in accessing public contracts, based on the assumption that the state will look for better alignment between private and public governance.

FIVE

Sustainable Ownership

Purpose

Corporate purpose determines beneficiary rights – that is, in whose interests the organization is expected to run. UK company law permits but does not require companies to define a specific corporate purpose in their articles of association.[1] If no such purpose is specified, it defaults, as discussed in Chapter Two, to a position that defines the fiduciary duty of the company directors in terms of promoting 'the success of the company for the benefit of its members as a whole' – that is, prioritizing its shareholders.[2] These default rules grant substantive beneficiary rights exclusively to the company's shareholders, and while this encourages an inclusive perspective by asking directors to have regard to other corporate stakeholders' interests, it does not actively prevent a company from adopting a financialized governance model, where its purpose becomes simply to extract profit for shareholders (see further Chapter Two).

For a contracting authority, this design offers little reassurance that the supplier company will not act opportunistically where it is in the shareholders' interest to do so. Of course, companies may nonetheless publish a commitment, perhaps in a public statement on their website, to delivering public

---

[1]   Section 172(2) Companies Act 2006.

[2]   Section 172(1) Companies Act 2006.

services. Serco,[3] for instance, identifies 'a set of four values – Trust, Care, Innovation, Pride – that shape our individual behaviours and hence the way the company behaves' and commits to creating 'innovative solutions that make positive impact and address some of the most urgent and complex challenges facing the modern world'.[4] Importantly, however, these are 'soft' commitments only and have no impact on the legal design of the organization, nor are they enforceable. Firms wishing, under UK law, to commit to a wider corporate purpose have several options. They may choose to incorporate their venture under a tailored corporate form available for certain social and community enterprises – for example, as a community interest company (see Box 5.1), a cooperative society or community benefit society, or in some cases an adapted company limited by guarantee (which may have members but has no shareholders). They may alternatively choose to incorporate as company limited by shares but, again, adapt this format to suit their mission by defining and incorporating a tailored purpose clause for their venture into the company's articles of association, thus imposing on company directors a legal duty to promote and prioritize the defined corporate purpose. The purpose clause may be protected from future change in the organization – that is, 'locked into' its corporate governance model – for example, by incorporating additional protection clauses into the corporate constitution. A constitutional 'supermajority' clause is a relatively safe but not risk-free option to lock in

---

[3]   As discussed in Chapter Two, Serco, a multinational public corporation, is an important strategic provider to the UK government in multiple public service sectors. In the past, the company's failures in public service delivery have attracted public attention.

[4]   See Serco's home page (www.serco.com/uk) and about page (www.serco.com/uk/about/culture-and-values), respectively. [Accessed 25 April 2024].

purpose.[5] A multiple-class share structure is an alternative or supplementary option (this may, for example, grant shareholders with longer tenure a gradual increase in voting rights to reward their long-term commitment to the firm).[6] A golden share model can also have a lock-in effect where a third party (typically a non-profit organization) holds a veto over any future changes to the purpose clause.[7]

From the perspective of a contracting authority, choosing a corporate partner committed to a purpose beyond shareholder value provides some reassurance that its governance model creates enough space for its directors and mangers to accommodate certain non-financial factors relevant to delivering public value, such as consistency and quality of service, without fear of being held accountable by shareholders for underperforming. In purposeful governance, there may even be room for organizational values not dissimilar to a public service ethos or, at least, values that we can expect to align with that ethos more closely than those of companies that are run to prioritize their shareholders; such values may be evident in efforts to incentivize the workforce delivering the public service not to lower service standards

---

[5]   Boeger, N. (2021) *Amending UK Company Law for a Regenerative Economy* [online], Institute of Directors, Available from: https://betterbusinessact. org/wp-content/uploads/2021/05/IoD-CG-Centre-Amending-UK-Company-Law.pdf [Accessed 27 February 2024].

[6]   Mayer, C. (2014) *Firm Commitment: Why the Corporation is Failing Us and How to Restore Trust in It*, Oxford: Oxford University Press.

[7]   Hogan Lovells (2015) *Going for Gold: How Golden Shares Can Help Lock in Mission for Social Enterprises*, Report prepared for Big Society Capital [online], Available from: www.hoganlovells.com/~/media/hogan-love lls/pdf/publication/4878744v1golden-share-report-final-formlwdli b01_pdf.pdf [Accessed 27 February 2024]. For a recent example, see the 'mission lock' incorporated into the company Tony's Chocolonely – Tony's Chocolonely (2023) 'Tony's mission lock' [online], June, Available from: https://tonyschocolonely.com/int/en/our-story/serious-stateme nts/tonys-mission-lock [Accessed 4 March 2024].

exploitatively where contractual gaps or incumbency might otherwise offer opportunities that would enable this. On the other hand, in attempting to *blend* a purpose clause with a continued (tempered) commitment to capital – seeking to integrate both purpose and profit into the governance model – some corporate organizations become vulnerable to new governance problems. For directors, the balancing of purpose and profit is a profound governance challenge, especially in situations where pursuing purpose can hardly be framed as a business case win-win – that is, a situation where the pursuit of purpose can also improve profit by, for example, creating reputational gains. In the delivery of public service contracts, those win-wins can be rare. Prioritizing service quality, for example, especially for non-contractible service elements that are hard to measure, simply may not yield any discernible long-term win in reputational terms, but instead present directors with a hard choice between offering better delivery or doing commercially better, weighing opportunities to economize quality to ensure commercial viability and success against delivering first-best service quality. Even where directors are strongly committed to prioritizing purpose, they will likely face uncomfortable questions from investors, stakeholders and, potentially, their contracting authority. These are, as in every firm, difficult governance decisions to take, but in these dual-purpose organizations, the risk that they may cause priorities to drift is particularly real.[8] Distinguishing the means and the ends of corporate governance in these situations – with regard to the role of purpose or profit – can quickly become very blurred here.[9]

---

[8] Ebrahim, A., Battilana, J. and Mair, J. (2014) 'The governance of social enterprises: mission drift and accountability challenges in hybrid organizations', *Research in Organizational Behavior*, 34: 81–100.

[9] On the related issue of 'purpose washing' or 'woke washing' of purposeful brands, see Vredenburg, J., Kapitan, S., Spry, A. and Kemper, J.A. (2020)

Contracting authorities should, therefore, reflect carefully on what kind of purpose commitment they would want to ideally see in a provider organization, bearing in mind that these may vary greatly depending not only on the provider's corporate legal form but also on the rationale that leads the organization to incorporate this commitment. A constitutional purpose clause may be framed as an unequivocal or discretionary obligation, a difference that determines whether, for directors, the pursuit of purpose *may* or *must* take priority over profit. Examples of alternative corporate ownership forms in the privatized UK water sector illustrate this difference. For instance, the corporate provider Welsh Water, which is run as a non-profit-distributing company limited by guarantee, has incorporated a sustainability pledge into its corporate purpose to 'provide high quality and better value drinking water and environmental services, so as to enhance the well-being of [our] customers and the communities [we serve], both now and for generations to come'.[10] Anglian Water, which is run as a profit-distributing company limited by shares, has committed 'to conduct its business and operations for the benefit of members as a whole while delivering long term value for its customers, the region and the communities it serves and seeking positive outcomes for the environment and society'.[11] Both companies refer in their commitment to the specific communities they serve. The difference of course is that in the case of Anglian Water, the commitment towards

---

'Brands taking a stand: authentic brand activism or woke washing?', *Journal of Public Policy and Marketing*, 39(4): 444–460.

[10] Glas Cymru Holdings Cyfyngedig [Welsh Water] (2019) *Articles of Association* [online], pt 2A, Available from: https://corporate.dwrcymru.com/en/about-us/governance/articles-of-association [Accessed 27 February 2024].

[11] Anglian Water Services Limited (undated) *Articles of Association* [online], Purpose and nature of company (A), Available from: www.anglianwater.co.uk/siteassets/household/about-us/articles-of-association.pdf [Accessed 27 February 2024].

'customers, the region and the communities' is expected to be balanced against the 'benefit of members as a whole' – that is, its financial shareholders. Meanwhile, in the case of Welsh Water, which has no financial shareholders, no such balancing is anticipated. While directors will still be expected to govern the business to ensure its commercial success and service any existing debt, they can remain unconcerned about distributing profit to shareholders.

Incorporating a specific social purpose – for example, to serve a distinct regional community, as in the case of these privatized water companies – is something that private companies may find more difficult where they bid for public service contracts more widely and repeatedly. These are typically 'companies with a more commercial business model and a less narrow geographical scope (and thus a sense of belonging) who operate in more competitive, liquid and global markets'.[12] However, for such companies too, it is perfectly possible in principle to incorporate a relevant purpose commitment into their ownership design which modifies beneficiary rights, introducing obligations for directors to prioritize interests other than their financial investors, although these would usually be more generic, less specific in scope and less likely to be linked to a certain community than the earlier examples. At its most generic, a commercial company might simply commit to prioritizing any productive purpose over profit. Such a clause is purely designed to temper the objective to prioritize shareholder value, pivoting the company further away from a financialized governance model and towards a sustainable corporate governance model. In principle, to express this in its ownership design only requires the company

---

[12] Jones, C., Metzner, M. and Stroehle, J.C. (2021) *Welsh Water: A Model for the Purposeful Ownership of a Utility?* Economics of Mutuality Forum Vase Studies [online], Saïd Business School, University of Oxford, January, p 14, Available from: www.sbs.ox.ac.uk/sites/default/files/2021-04/welsh-water-case-study.pdf [Accessed 27 February 2024].

to incorporate into its constitution a commitment to create something of value that is socially useful, and this may simply be producing high-quality goods to help consumers. But to ensure the commitment is to create *sustainable* value, more often companies that commit to a purpose express this as a commitment to wider society and stakeholders, including to take account of the impact of their activities on the environment and on society.

Certified B Corps, for example, tend to remain fully profit distributing, but adjust their constitution to take account of wider concerns of their stakeholders and society. In the UK, this (private) certification mechanism requires of any company wishing to use the label 'B Corp' that they identify in their articles of association that the 'objects of the Company are to promote the success of the Company: (i) for the benefit of its members as a whole; and (ii) through its business and operations, to have a material positive impact on (a) society and (b) the environment, taken as a whole'.[13] These companies then become rather open-ended dual-purpose organizations, assuming responsibilities towards their non-investing beneficiaries while also retaining financial responsibilities towards investors.[14] Inevitably, this impacts on their governance, requiring some delicate balancing as directors are now bestowed a rather wide scope of discretion in weighing the interests of investors and other beneficiaries (stakeholders and society). Given the open-ended nature of the purpose clause, the interests of stakeholders and society take no clear priority over shareholders as they would, for example, in a community business incorporated as a UK

---

[13] B Lab United Kingdom (2024) *The 'Legal Requirement' for a B Corp in the UK* [online], paragraph 2, Available from: https://bcorporation.uk/ b-corp-certification/how-to-certify-as-a-b-corp/legal-requirement/ #guide [Accessed 27 February 2024].

[14] Brakman Reiser, D. (2010) 'Blended enterprise and the dual mission dilemma', *Vermont Law Review*, 35: 105–116.

community interest company – a tailored legal form with a clear legal assurance 'that profits and assets would be used to deliver the objectives of the company ... for the benefit of the public and the community' (see also Box 5.1).[15] B Corp certification, on the other hand, does not create the same level of priority. In effect, it simply creates a safe space for directors to acknowledge and act on their commitment to non–investing beneficiaries without fear of being held legally accountable by their shareholders for underperforming. The B Corp has been expressly designed to 'reduce the liability for Directors and Officers by creating legal protection (called "safe harbor") for them to take into consideration the interests of multiple stakeholders when making decisions, particularly when considering financing and liquidity scenarios'.[16] B Corp certification does not require the company to formally restrict its right to distribute profits to shareholders, nor in fact is B Corp status entrenched; certification can be reversed at any time – for example, if the company feels that it needs to revert to a more commercial operation.[17] It is, in other

---

[15] Community Interest Companies, volume 402, debated on 26 March 2003, Minister for Women Patricia Hewitt MP, column 13WS, Available from: https://hansard.parliament.uk/commons/2003-03-26/debates/a94bb9d8-58ed-4a66-84c7-8a4c791407a0/CommunityInterestCompan ies [Accessed 27 February 2024]. See also NHS Providers (undated) 'Community interest companies' [online], Available from: https://nhspr oviders.org/state-of-the-provider-sector-05-18/community-interest-companies [Accessed 27 February 2024].

[16] B Impact Assessment Support Portal (2023) 'What is the legal requirement for my company and why do I need to meet it?' [online], updated 18 September, Available from: https://kb.bimpactassessment.net/support/solutions/articles/43000015941-what-is-the-legal-requ irement-for-my-company-and-why-do-i-need-to-meet-it- [Accessed 27 February 2024].

[17] See in relation to B Corp, the story of BrewDog: Anjili, R. (2023) 'The struggle for the soul of the B Corp movement', *The Financial Times* [online], 19 February, Available from: www.ft.com/content/0b632709-afda-4bdc-a6f3-bb0b02eb5a62 [Accessed 27 February 2024].

words, a rather mild and potentially temporary adjustment to the company's design and governance – arguably, only a nod towards a sustainable corporate design. For some contracting authorities and some contracts, this may not provide sufficient reassurance of sustainable ownership design. For others, however, it might. As a typically profit-distributing corporate format, it accommodates access to capital investment which is a key factor for highly capitalized public service projects. Similarly, in an outsourcing context, what matters chiefly is that corporate features apply for the duration of the outsourcing contract – the possibility of reversing a purpose clause and B Corp certification may, therefore, be secondary for a contracting authority. It may also be possible in some cases to use contractual devices to supplement these requirements – for example a contractual penalty clause in the public services contract if the provider falls short of the governance commitment.[18] From a contracting authority's point of view, even the B Corp's relatively light touch dual-purpose commitment could therefore become a relevant concern in how best to manage various outsourcing risks.[19]

---

[18] An analogy may be drawn with the availability of contractual 'green pills' designed to enable firms to make their 'climate commitments credible by endogenizing incentives to meet climate targets' – Armour, J., Enriques, L. and Wetzer, T. (2022) *Green Pills: Making Corporate Climate Commitments Credible*, European Corporate Governance Institute Working Paper No 657/2022 [online], 1 December, p 1, Available from: http://dx.doi.org/10.2139/ssrn.4190268 [Accessed 27 February 2024].

[19] See, for example, the Welsh Government's express reference, in its analysis of the provision of social care services, to 'local private ownership that supports a triple bottom line – namely, a concern for the wider community, the environment and workers, alongside the pursuit of profit' – Welsh Government (2022) *Toolkit for Insourcing in Wales* [online], 19 December, p 34, Available from: www.gov.wales/sites/default/files/pdf-versions/2022/12/1/1671444331/a-toolkit-for-insourcing-in-wales.pdf [Accessed 27 February 2024].

It is possible to blend specific and generic aspects of purpose. This is what happens in many public benefit corporations, which is a format that already exists in several jurisdictions, including the US, but not currently in the UK. In the US, for example, the statutory format requires for-profit companies, in order to incorporate as a benefit corporation, to include into their constitution a commitment

> that is intended to produce a public benefit or public benefits and to operate in a responsible and sustainable manner. To that end, a public benefit corporation shall be managed in a manner that balances the stockholders' pecuniary interests, the best interests of those materially affected by the corporation's conduct, and the public benefit or public benefits identified in its certificate of incorporation.[20]

Both the self-defined specific public benefit and the commitment to stakeholder interests defined generically by statute are relevant in this format, which has, for this very reason, repeatedly found reference in recent discussions as a potential model for private companies delivering public services in the UK. For example, the now abandoned draft Thames Water (Public Benefit Corporation) Bill would have forced Thames Water as the largest (and, therefore, least geographically embedded) commercial provider of privatized water services to reincorporate as a public benefit corporation with a purpose 'to consider public policy benefits, including reducing leaks and sewage dumping, as well as returns for shareholders'.[21]

---

[20] Delaware Corporations Code, §362, Available from: https://delcode. delaware.gov/title8/c001/sc15/ [Accessed 27 February 2024].

[21] UK Parliament (2023) Thames Water (Public Benefit Corporation) Bill, Private Members' Bill (Presentation Bill), originated in the House of Commons [online], updated 2 November, Available from: https:// bills.parliament.uk/bills/3483 [Accessed 27 February 2024]. Liberal

The Bill was introduced in response to repeated serious issues resulting from financialized corporate governance in the company, described as 'deep-rooted problems of persistent poor performance and too much debt'.[22] Meanwhile the chief executive officer of another troubled UK private water provider recently proposed, following repeated outsourcing failures, to 'repurpose' utilities providers 'into a new breed of declared social purpose companies – companies that remain privately owned, which absolutely can (and should) make a profit, but ones that also have a special duty to take a long-term view'.[23] Other commentators too have advocated the creation of a new category of public benefit company in Britain that would 'write into its constitution that its purpose is the delivery of public benefit to which profit-making is subordinate. For instance, a water company's purpose would be to deliver the best water as cheaply as possible and not siphon off excessive dividends through a tax haven.'[24] On the other hand, there is a question as to whether, insofar as these companies would remain profit

Democrats (2023) 'Parliamentary Bill tabled to "rip up" Thames Water and begin industry reform' [online], 28 June, Available from: www.libd ems.org.uk/press/release/parliamentary-bill-tabled-to-rip-up-thames-water-and-begin-industry-reform [Accessed 27 February 2024]. The Bill also proposed to limit the payment of dividends until a plan is in place to cut the corporation's debt, and to require membership of the corporation's board to include representatives of local environment groups.

[22] Black, D. (2023) 'Thames, debt and water sector finance', *Ofwat* [online], 24 July, Available from: www.ofwat.gov.uk/thames-debt-and-water-sec tor-finance/ [Accessed 27 February 2024].

[23] Lawson, A. (2023) 'Severn Trent chief proposes "social purpose" water firms amid utilities crisis', *The Guardian* [online], 30 June, Available from: www.theguardian.com/business/2023/jun/30/severn-trent-chief-social-purpose-water-firms-utilities-crisis-liv-garfield-thames-water-lab our-renationalisation [Accessed 26 February 2024].

[24] Hutton, W. (2018) 'We can undo privatisation. And it won't cost us a penny', *The Guardian* [online], 9 January, Available from: www.theguard ian.com/commentisfree/2018/jan/09/nationalise-rail-gas-water-privat ely-owned [Accessed 27 February 2024].

distributing and shareholder 'rights to votes and dividends would remain unimpaired',[25] contracting authorities and regulators could be sufficiently assured that this new format can prevent a drift (back) into financialized corporate governance.[26]

Box 5.1

The connection between community purpose and the private delivery of public services was made explicit in the introduction in 2005 of a designated corporate form: the community interest company.[a] Incorporation as community interest company creates a different type of purpose-led business to a certified B Corp (or, outside the UK, a public benefit corporation). Broadly speaking, the former operates as VCSE, while the latter is typically a more commercial and looser dual-purpose enterprise outside the VCSE frame. The community interest company was introduced inter alia as a corporate form suited to improve the private delivery of local public services, with the legislation setting up a dedicated regulator to oversee its statutory features. As the relevant minister explained at the time, though this corporate form was not expected to provide 'essential public services in core sectors such as hospitals and schools', it was developed 'to meet the needs of local communities, complementing core Government services in areas such as childcare provision, social housing, leisure and community transport'; crucially, its key features would provide assurance 'that profits and assets would be used to deliver the objectives of the company ... for the benefit of the public and the community'.[b]

A community interest company, in order to be incorporated, must set out a defined community interest purpose in its articles of association, which may be changed only with regulatory approval, requiring it to

---

[25] Lawson, A. (2023) 'Severn Trent chief proposes "social purpose" water firms amid utilities crisis', *The Guardian* [online], 30 June, Available from: www.theguardian.com/business/2023/jun/30/severn-trent-chief-social-purpose-water-firms-utilities-crisis-liv-garfield-thames-water-labour-renationalisation [Accessed 26 February 2024].

[26] Ebrahim, A., Battilana, J. and Mair, J. (2014) 'The governance of social enterprises: mission drift and accountability challenges in hybrid organizations', *Research in Organizational Behavior*, 34: 81–100.

demonstrate that a reasonable person would consider it delivers a benefit to the community.[c] Annual reporting on these issues to the regulator is required. The statutory regime further imposes a legally mandated asset lock clause on all community interest companies whereby assets may only be transferred out of the business if there is a transfer at full market value or to another specified or approved asset-locked body or to benefit the community. Where a community interest company issues shares (which they may), a statutory cap is imposed on the level of dividend that can lawfully be distributed to shareholders. These legal restrictions are designed to lock in and preserve the value of the company's assets and profits while also providing for some flexibility to access share capital and provide return to investors. A community interest company can still use its own assets as loan collateral, even if it means that assets may have to be sold to repay debt.

The role of the regulator forms a central piece of this legal framework, designed to ensure that both community benefit and commercial components of the community interest company are adequately accounted for. To strike such a balance, the regulator operates a light touch regime in terms of the intensity and extent of their reviews and investigations, enforcement and sanctioning. The point is to enable organizations to operate relatively freely in a commercial sense, intervening only when there is clear concern that this will undermine their community interest mission. The organization is thus subject to the same reporting requirements to Companies House as commercial companies. In addition, every community interest company is under a legal obligation deliver an annual community interest company report detailing its activities for the public record, including details of asset transfers, dividend payments, directors' remuneration and stakeholder involvement. The regulator files all reports on the public register.[d]

a   See the Companies (Audit, Investigations and Community Enterprise) Act 2004 and Community Interest Company Regulations 2005.
b   Community Interest Companies, volume 402, debated on Wednesday 26 March, Patricia Hewitt, column 14WS, Available from: https://hansard.par liament.uk/commons/2003-03-26/debates/a94bb9d8-58ed-4a66-84c7-8a4c791407a0/CommunityInterestCompanies [Accessed 13 April 2024]. See also NHS Providers (2018), 'Community Interest Companies', [online], Available from: https://nhsproviders.org/state-of-the-provider-sector-05-18/community-interest-companies [Accessed 25 April 2024].
c   Office of the Regulator of Community Interest Companies (2024) 'Community Interest Companies Guidance', [online] 9 February, Available

from: https://www.gov.uk/government/publications/community-interest-companies-how-to-form-a-cic/community-interest-companies-guidance-chapters [Accessed 27 February 2024].

d   Office of the Regulator of Community Interest Companies (2020) 'CIC34: community interest company report', [online] 2 June, Available from: https://www.gov.uk/government/publications/form-cic34-community-interest-company-report [Accessed 27 February 2024].

Power

Direct control over a company is vested in the board of directors, which in the UK and most other jurisdictions is collectively responsible 'for the management of the company's business'.[27] Members (in the case of a company limited by shares, the shareholders), on the other hand, hold certain rights of intervention to hold company directors to account, including the right to appoint and dismiss the directors and, typically, to 'direct the directors to take, or refrain from taking, specified action'.[28] Unless a company's articles of association provide differently, the internal division of powers aligns with the default legal

---

[27]   See Companies House (2018) 'Model articles for private companies limited by shares' [online], 18 September, Article 3, Available from: www.gov.uk/government/publications/model-articles-for-private-companies-limited-by-shares/model-articles-for-private-companies-limited-by-shares [Accessed 27 February 2024].

[28]   Companies House (2018) 'Model articles for private companies limited by shares' [online], updated 18 September, Article 4(1) (reserve rights), Available from: www.gov.uk/government/publications/model-articles-for-private-companies-limited-by-shares/model-articles-for-private-companies-limited-by-shares [Accessed 27 February 2024]; see also Article 17 (appointment of director). See also sections 168 and 169 Companies Act 2006 (dismissal of director). For a more comprehensive list of shareholders' rights of intervention, see Moore, M. and Petrin, M. (2017) *Corporate Governance: Law, Regulation and Theory*, London: Palgrave, p 83. Note that Moore and Petrin also distinguish between control and information rights, such as access to disclosure. The exercise of any of these rights requires a member vote by a specified majority.

provisions on corporate purpose and fiduciary duties discussed in the previous section of this chapter. That is, the board as its primary decision-making organ is accountable to the very shareholders whose interests it is expected to prioritize. The default rules in UK company law do not confer any significant control rights on non-shareholding stakeholders, bar a cursory provision of workforce engagement on company boards for large public companies.[29] Only shareholders hold various powers in company law to enforce their rights against the company.[30] Given that, typically, the link between the shareholder and the company is the financial equity investment, the default position effectively prioritizes those financial investors' governance rights over those of non-shareholding stakeholders.

Where companies are expected to deliver public services, contracting authorities may wish to see more power in the hands of those stakeholders whose interest in the company is determined by factors other than their capital contributions, including employees, service recipients and other groups indirectly impacted by the service in question, such as local communities or even the wider public. Any organization has the possibility of vesting some powers in the organization in these stakeholders as long as that is what its members wish and its constitution and relevant ancillary documentation provide for it. Once again, to do this, they may either incorporate provisions to that effect into the articles of association of a traditional company, supported by supplementary

---

[29] 'For engagement with the workforce, one or a combination of the following methods should be used: a director appointed from the workforce; a formal workforce advisory panel; or a designated non-executive director' – Financial Reporting Council (2024) *UK Corporate Governance Code* [online], January, Section 1, Provision 5, Available from: https://media.frc.org.uk/documents/UK_Corporate_Governanc e_Code_2024_kRCm5ss.pdf [Accessed 27 February 2024]. Data suggest that the first option is rarely selected, if at all.

[30] See the derivative action (Part 11 Companies Act 2006), unfair prejudice petition (Part 30 Companies Act 2006) and winding up petition (section 122 Insolvency Act 1986).

documentation as needed (for example, a consumer or works council statute). Or they may choose an alternative legal form that by default vests control rights in stakeholders – for example, incorporating under the UK legal regime for cooperative societies and community benefit societies. The legal design of different corporate organizations can, whether by choice or default, reflect very different types of stakeholder governance, including in terms of scope (what stakeholders may hold control rights) and character (the nature and level of their power). Exactly what kind of version might be helpful to improve an outsourcing relationship and reduce the possibility of problems in public contracting depends on a range of factors, including the outsourced services in question and the character of the organizations that bid to provide it. It also, importantly, depends on the contracting authority itself having a clear idea of what exactly it is trying to achieve by seeking out stakeholder governance in the organization.

It may relate to improving the quality of service delivery. Where experienced and relevant stakeholders have a governance role in the organization delivering them, this creates an opportunity for those stakeholders to provide input into delivery methods and design of the services in question, all the more important if there are complexities and uncertainties that cannot be predicted by the contract in advance but must be determined and resolved over the course of its delivery. By exercising governance powers in the supplier organization, stakeholders may improve services and avoid problems, thereby 'harnessing the assets and resources of users and communities to achieve better outcomes and lower cost' and reassuring the contracting authority that it is creating value for those stakeholders and for society.[31] In addition, stakeholder control can be helpful in providing supplementary accountability

---

[31] Bovaird, T. and Löffler, E. (2012) 'From engagement to co-production: how users and communities contribute to public services', in V. Pestoff, T. Brandsen and B. Verschure (eds) *New Public Governance, the Third Sector and Co-Production*, Abingdon: Routledge, pp 35–60, p 36.

and protection against exploitation of public contracting obligations by creating a decision-making framework inside the provider organization where different perspectives can control one another. The contracting authority, able to trust stakeholders to address situations where the private provider might otherwise be tempted to act opportunistically vis-à-vis the public contracting partner, may then more confidently draft contract specifications that incorporate greater flexibility to resolve details in the course of its delivery, creating room for relational contracting. This assumes, however, that stakeholder accountability can be made effective – that when problems are identified, stakeholders hold intervention rights to apply pressure on the organization and effect change if needed.[32] It also assumes that they are prepared to exercise those powers. Unless clear incentives to do so are in place, even high levels of formal stakeholder control 'may not readily translate into high levels of engagement and participation'.[33]

Stakeholder powers in the provider organization may amount to full membership. Such is the case in mutual firms where members are, for example, customers, employees, suppliers or community groups, and they hold the power directly to control decision making in the firm (see Box 5.2). Some mutual firms vest membership in multiple stakeholder groups.[34] In

---

[32] Cooper, S. (2018) 'The case of Triodos Bank', in N. Boeger and C. Villiers (eds) *Shaping the Corporate Landscape: Between Corporate Reform and Enterprise Diversity*, Oxford: Hart Publishing, pp 233 – 251.

[33] Vickers, I., Lyon, F., Sepulveda, L. and Brennan, G. (2021) *Public Service Mutuals: Transforming How Services Are Delivered through Social Enterprise and Democratic Governance?* [online], Centre for Enterprise and Economic Development Research and Middlesex University, in cooperation with Social Enterprise UK, January, p 6, Available from: https://assets.publish ing.service.gov.uk/media/630f64978fa8f544842c49b3/Public_Service_ Mutuals_Longitudinal_Case_Study.pdf [Accessed 27 February 2024].

[34] 'The Board of Directors shall be elected by and from the Co-operative's Members. The composition of the Board of Directors following the first annual general meeting shall be as follows: (a) Not more than ... User

the UK, for the past decade or so, the involvement of mutual organizations in the delivery of public services has been linked closely to the emergence of the public service mutuals (see further Chapter Four) in public procurement law and policy. Setting up the Mutuals Taskforce in 2011 to support their creation,[35] government introduced the public service mutual format mainly to enable public sector employees to spin out their work and set up an employee–owned social enterprise to deliver public services directly and independently, typically without distributing profit to private investors.[36] Because they deliver public services on a non–profit basis, the creation of public service mutuals 'meant that employee ownership was attached to social enterprise business models'.[37] It was the UK

Members; (b) Not more than … Employee Members; (c) Not more than … Producer Members; (d) Not more than … Consumer Members' – Cooperatives UK (2018) *Multi-Stakeholder Co-operative Model Rules* [online], paragraph 76, Available from: www.uk.coop/sites/default/files/2020-10/2014_multi-stakeholder_co-operative_0.pdf [Accessed 27 February 2024].

[35] See Mutuals Taskforce (2011) *Our Mutual Friends: Making the Case for Public Service Mutuals* [online], Available from: https://assets.publishing.service.gov.uk/media/5a79d29440f0b670a8025ad8/Our-Mutual-Friends.pdf [Accessed 27 February 2024]. Mutuals Taskforce (2012) 'Mutual and cooperative approaches to delivering local services', written evidence before the House of Commons Communities and Local Government Committee [online], May, Available from: https://publications.parliament.uk/pa/cm201213/cmselect/cmcomloc/112/112we08.htm [Accessed 27 February 2024].

[36] Francis Maude MP, Cabinet Office Minister at the time, described the government's 'plans to set public sector workers free, to let them take control of their organisations, turn them into mutuals and have more control and autonomy over how things are run' – Cabinet Office and the Rt Hon Lord Maude of Horsham (2010) 'Francis Maude speech unveiling new support for mutuals' [online], 17 November, Available from: www.gov.uk/government/speeches/francis-maude-speech-unveiling-new-support-for-mutuals [Accessed 27 February 2024].

[37] Pendleton, A., Robinson, A. and Nuttall, G. (2023) 'Employee ownership in the UK', *Journal of Participation and Employee Ownership*, 6(3): 194–214, p 199.

government that advocated at the time for the possibility to reserve contracts for public service mutuals under the (then) EU 'light touch' procurement legal regime to deliver mainly person–centred public services, facing down concerns that to do so could enable further privatization and be seen as 'a cynical exercise in public expenditure cuts'.[38] The new public procurement legislation continues to make available the possibility that contracting authorities can set aside contracts to deliver light touch services for public service mutuals when the relevant conditions are met (see further Chapter Four).[39] The definition of these mutual organizations under the new law reinforces their character as social economy (VCSE) organizations rather than as mutual firms in the wider economy.[40] In legal terms, over half of existing public service mutuals incorporate as asset–locked community interest companies or community benefit societies and identify primarily as a social enterprise – very few incorporate, for example, as a limited company.[41]

A different set of corporate organizations in mutual and employee ownership operate in the wider economy, where mutual ownership may not be linked to a particular social purpose other than a central idea of 'members putting

---

[38] UNISON (2013) *Mutual Benefit? Should Mutuals, Co-Operatives and Social Enterprises Deliver Public Services?* [online], p 32, Available from: www.unison.org.uk/content/uploads/2013/06/On–line–Catalogue199463.pdf [Accessed 27 February 2024].

[39] This is for a maximum duration of five years (provided the same organization has not been awarded a contract for three years prior).

[40] Section 33(6) PA2023 – here, a public service mutual is legally defined as a body that operates for the purpose of delivering public services, is run on a not-for-profit basis or provides for the distribution of profits only to members, and is under the management and control of its employees.

[41] Social Enterprise UK (2019) *Public Service Mutuals: The State of the Sector* [online], April, pp 7–8, Available from https://assets.publishing.service.gov.uk/media/5ffec084e90e0763a8db979c/Public_Service_Mutuals_-_The_State_of_the_Sector_2019_V2.pdf [Accessed 28 February 2024].

their resources together to satisfy their common needs'.[42] They may be set up as mutual societies, but they include a growing number of commercial companies whose shares are owned, directly or via an employee ownership trust, by their employees.[43] The legal structure in these employee–owned firms remains a company limited by shares, but those are fully or majority owned for the benefit of the company's employees. In particular, the indirect employee ownership structure via a trust enjoys growing popularity, directly in response to targeted tax–incentivized government support.[44] The John Lewis Partnership, as a widely known example of this structure, is owned by a trust on behalf of its employees (or 'partners'). The trustee, a private limited company, holds all shares with voting and economic rights in the trading firm, John Lewis Partnership plc, for the benefit of its partners, who thus receive a share in the partnership's profit. A governance structure provides for partners to elect members of a Partnership Council, which in turn elects members of the firm's Partnership Board. The key management role is

---

[42] Sheperd, J. (2023) *Mutual Understanding: The Modern Mutual Sector and How to Support It* [online], Social Market Foundation, June, p 12, Available from: www.smf.co.uk/wp-content/uploads/2023/06/Mutual-understanding-June-2023.pdf [Accessed 28 February 2024].

[43] Sheperd notes that 'while all co–operatives are mutuals, not all mutuals are co–operatives' – Sheperd, J. (2023) *Mutual Understanding: The Modern Mutual Sector and How to Support It* [online], Social Market Foundation, June, p 13, Available from: www.smf.co.uk/wp-content/uploads/2023/06/Mutual-understanding-June-2023.pdf [Accessed 28 February 2024].

[44] Pendleton, A., Robinson, A. and Nuttall, G. (2023) 'Employee ownership in the UK', *Journal of Participation and Employee Ownership*, 6(3): 194–214, p 199. McDougall, M. (2022) 'UK businesses turn to employee-ownership at record rates', *The Financial Times* [online], 8 December, Available from: www.ft.com/content/27e25bf9-e1a0-445d-aa90-339eacb0c686 [Accessed 28 February 2024]. Staton, B. (2020) 'UK government services group Seetec becomes employee owned', *The Financial Times* [online], 10 January, Available from: www.ft.com/content/c0e13312-338f-11ea-9703-eea0cae3f0de [Accessed 28 February 2024].

held by John Lewis Partnership's chair, who is not elected but appointed by the outgoing chair.

In a public outsourcing context, a mutual ownership structure – going beyond the distinct and legally defined public service mutual – can have important governance implications in the supplier organization. Stakeholder members are directly involved in decisions that affect them and the firm, having 'a real voice in the organisation' and, under company law, some rights of legal enforcement against the company.[45] Mutual firms, therefore, operate differently from dual-purpose organizations, such as B Corp-certified commercial firms, which do not usually confer any enforcement rights on stakeholders even though they commit company directors to balancing investors' interests against wider stakeholders' interests. In effect, only investors, as shareholders, can take action against a commercially owned B Corp where they consider that directors fall short in exercising these duties.[46] In mutually owned firms, on the other hand, by virtue of being members, even non-investing stakeholders in the firm hold these control rights. This of course is exactly the reason why, in the context of public service outsourcing, mutual ownership might offer a solution to current problems of exploitation, especially where commercial providers operate financialized corporate governance models.[47]

[45] Ham, C. and Ellins, J. (2010) 'Employee ownership in the NHS', *British Medical Journal*, 341: c6759. doi: 10.1136/bmj.c6759

[46] 'Adopting the B Corp legal framework will, however, give shareholders additional rights to hold Directors and Officers accountable for taking into consideration these same interests when making decisions --and that, of course, is the whole point' – B Impact Assessment Support Portal (2023) 'What is the legal requirement for my company and why do I need to meet it?' [online], updated 18 September, Available from: https://kb.bimpactassessment.net/support/solutions/articles/4300 0015941-what-is-the-legal-requirement-for-my-company-and-why-do-i-need-to-meet-it- [Accessed 27 February 2024].

[47] Birchall, J. (2002) *A Mutual Trend: How to Run Rail and Water in the Public Interest* [online], New Economics Foundation, Available from:

Short of membership, stakeholders may be given the opportunity to exercise decision-making power as non-members – for example, by participating in, or formally engaging with, the board of directors of a corporate organization. To provide for this is a considerable step for a commercial firm. Stakeholder representation on commercial company boards has, in the UK at least, gained little traction despite efforts more generally to improve diversity in the boardroom.[48] Typically associated with a co-determination model of corporate governance that prevails in other jurisdictions,[49] large UK companies in particular continue to see risks in overcomplicating the dynamics of the boardroom by incorporating stakeholders into the board.[50] One concern seems to be that to do so may render governance more complex without guaranteeing that companies will genuinely operate more sustainably – for example, because employee stakeholders might 'have as much incentive as do stockholders to pollute the environment or to sell shoddy products to one-time

https://dspace.stir.ac.uk/bitstream/1893/3359/1/A%20Mutual%20tr end.pdf [Accessed 28 February 2024].

[48] Ashtana, A. and Walker, P. (2016) 'Theresa May: I won't force companies to appoint workers to their boards', *The Guardian* [online], 21 November, Available from: www.theguardian.com/business/2016/nov/21/theresa-may-force-firms-appoint-workers-boards-cbi [Accessed 28 February 2024].

[49] McGaughey, E. (2016) 'The codetermination bargains: the history of German corporate and labor law', *Columbia Journal of European Law*, 23: 135–179. Strine, L.E. Jr., Kovvali, A. and Williams, O.O. (2021) 'Lifting labor's voice: a principled path toward greater worker voice and power within American corporate governance', Faculty Scholarship at Penn Carey Law, 2256, Available from: https://scholarship.law.upenn.edu/faculty_scholarship/2256 [Accessed 28 February 2024].

[50] Rees, C. and Briône, P. (2021) *Workforce Engagement and the UK Corporate Governance Code: A Review of Company Reporting and Practice* [online], Royal Holloway, University of London, May, Available from: https://media.frc.org.uk/documents/FRC_Workforce_Engagement_Report_May_2021.pdf [Accessed 28 February 2024].

purchasers'.[51] Not even B Corps, despite their purpose commitment to a more sustainable governance model, are expected to have stakeholders on their boards be certified, and nor is direct stakeholder representation a legal requirement for incorporation as a community interest company despite their legally required community purpose. Companies wishing to confer these direct control rights on stakeholders must instead do so as an active choice and incorporate this into their governance model.[52] Where companies provide public services on behalf of the state, the parameters that determine these choices arguably change insofar as from the perspective of a contracting authority, seeking out providers that feature stakeholder co-determination in their boardroom may offer an important additional layer of accountability over the successful delivery of a public outsourcing contract. And even if stakeholder governance is not mandated inside the boardroom, stakeholder engagement may at least be provided in corporate fora beyond the boardroom (as a separate panel, committee or council, for example). These may be set up contractually relating to an individual outsourcing project,[53] but their integration into the legal design and governance

---

[51] Dent, G.W. Jr. (2008) 'Stakeholder governance: a bad idea getting worse', *Case Western Reserve Law Review*, 58(4): 1107–1144, p 1114, Available from: https://scholarlycommons.law.case.edu/caselrev/vol58/iss4/11 [Accessed 28 February 2024].

[52] In relation to companies listed on the London Stock Exchange, see the provisions on 'workforce engagement' in Section 1, Provision 5 of the UK Corporate Governance Code 2024 – Financial Reporting Council (2024) *UK Corporate Governance Code* [online], January, Available from: https://media.frc.org.uk/documents/UK_Corporate_Governanc e_Code_2024_kRCm5ss.pdf [Accessed 27 February 2024].

[53] For an example, see in relation to the contract between the Scottish transport ministry and Serco plc over the Northern Isles Ferry Service: *Schedule 23 – Stakeholder and Community Engagement Delivery Plan*, Available from: www.transport.gov.scot/media/51354/schedule-23-stakeholder-and-community-engagement-delivery-plan-redacted. pdf [Accessed 28 February 2024].

model of the corporate organization reduces the need for further-reaching contractual specification. In community interest companies, for example, some community stakeholder engagement is expected 'as essential for the company to learn and understand how it is meeting community need and how it can improve and develop'; thus it forms part of the community interest reporting requirement.[54] Contracting authorities may however also expect commercial supplier firms to have equivalent measures in place, insisting, for example, that they 'would engage directly with consumer challenge groups whose mandate is to be a sounding board for consumer interests'.[55]

Box 5.2

Welsh Water is an example of mutual ownership in community hands. Incorporated as a company limited by guarantee, the firm admits non-shareholding members 'to ensure that the business remains focused on its primary purpose of providing high quality water and sewerage services to the communities served by [the company]'; it emphasizes that in order to fulfil this corporate governance role, 'Membership is personal and Members are not appointed to represent any particular group or stakeholder interest. Members do not receive a fee.'[a] The company's board of directors is accountable to members, with the latter expected to scrutinize its 'performance against commercial, regulatory and other targets, as well as against water industry benchmarks for quality of service and cost efficiency'. The company explains that the role of members 'is similar to that of a shareholder in a public limited

---

54 Burrough, J., Deacon, M., Bates Wells Braithwaite, CIC Association, National Council of Voluntary Organisations and Social Enterprise UK (2015) *Governance for Community Interest Companies: A Practical Framework*, [online], p 5, Available from: www.voscur.org/sites/default/files/Governa nce%20for%20Community%20Interest%20Companies.pdf [Accessed 28 February 2024].

55 Hutton, W. (2018) 'We can undo privatisation. And it won't cost us a penny', *The Guardian* [online], 9 January, Available from: www.theguard ian.com/commentisfree/2018/jan/09/nationalise-rail-gas-water-privat ely-owned [Accessed 27 February 2024].

company, save that a Member has no financial interest in the Group. Members perform this corporate governance role by receiving regular reports on the Group's activities and performance and by participating in Members' conferences and in general meetings.'[b] The board, led by an independent chair, is responsible for appointing the members 'on the basis of an appropriate combination of expertise, experience and capacity to contribute to these key governance roles'.[c]

a   Dŵr Cymru Welsh Water (undated) 'Our members' [online], Available from: https://corporate.dwrcymru.com/en/about-us/governance/our-members [Accessed 13 April 2024].

b   Glas Cymru Holdings Cyfyngedig [Welsh Water] (2017) *Policy and Procedure for the Selection and Appointment of the Members of Glas Cymru Holdings Cyfyngedig* [online], paragraph 5, Available from: https://corporate.dwrcymru.com/en/about-us/governance/our-members [Accessed 28 February 2024].

c   Glas Cymru Holdings Cyfyngedig [Welsh Water] (2017) *Policy and Procedure for the Selection and Appointment of the Members of Glas Cymru Holdings Cyfyngedig* [online], paragraph 9, Available from: https://corporate.dwrcymru.com/en/about-us/governance/our-members [Accessed 28 February 2024].

Profit

Profit–making in commercial companies is by legal design linked to the shareholders' economic rights in the organization. They can expect to receive returns on their capital investment as a result of either price appreciation of their shares or a dividend payment. The expectation of returns is what enables the company to attract capital investment in equity shares. On the other hand, alternative corporate designs (sometimes referred to as 'non–profit') impose constraints on the distribution of profits (see Box 5.3). In these organizations, while they are 'not barred from earning a profit', these earnings 'must be retained and devoted in their entirety to financing further production of services' rather than distributed to shareholders.[56] Economic rights in the organization are

---

[56] Hansmann, H.B. (1980) 'The role of nonprofit enterprise', *The Yale Law Journal*, 89(5): 835–901, p 838 (footnotes omitted).

here tempered to ensure its productive operation and purpose take priority.

In a public outsourcing context (see further Chapters One and Two), access to private capital in commercial firms can help support public capabilities, but it can also exacerbate risks that these providers, in seeking to prioritize profit that will drive up investor returns, act opportunistically vis-à-vis the public contracting partner. Rather than growing public capabilities, when corporate governance becomes driven by profit exclusively, its design ultimately is to extract more than sustain and generate public value. Contracting authorities will want to balance the benefits of outsourcing to profit-distributing firms against these risks, ensuring that investor return is not prioritized so far as to turn public contracting simply into a rent-seeking opportunity for the corporate organization. To do so they may seek out providers operating under a profit distribution constraint that reduces the risk of opportunistic behaviour.[57] Even if firms with a constraint on profit distribution 'might be expected to be slower in meeting increased demand and to be less efficient in their use of input than for-profit firms', their internal distribution constraint has the important governance advantage that 'those in charge are barred from taking home any resulting profits', creating fewer financial incentives for them to shirk on non-contractible quality obligations.[58] Therefore, the advantage of these providers, to conclude with

---

[57] Thornton, J. and Lecy, J. (2019) 'Good enough for government work? An incomplete contracts approach to the use of nonprofits in U.S. federal procurement', *Nonprofit Policy Forum*, 10(3): 1–18, p 2, Available from: https://ideas.repec.org/a/bpj/nonpfo/v10y2019i3p18n4.html [Accessed 28 February 2024]. Brown, L.K. and Troutt, E. (2004) 'Funding relations between nonprofits and government: a positive example', *Nonprofit and Voluntary Sector Quarterly*, 33(1): 5–27. Bennett, J. and Iossa, E. (2010) 'Contracting out public service provision to not-for-profit firms', *Oxford Economic Papers*, 62(4): 784–802.

[58] Hansmann, H.B. (1980) 'The role of nonprofit enterprise', *The Yale Law Journal*, 89(5): 835–901, p 844.

Hansmann, 'is that the discipline of the market is supplemented by the additional protection [of] the organisation's legal commitment to devote its entire earning to the production of services'.[59] Acknowledging that these 'diluted incentives for self-dealing may improve cooperation and result in more stable systems of mutually beneficial relationships', Thornton and Lecy find evidence in the US that an internal constraint on profit distribution offers 'a credible signal of goal alignment' between public authority and private provider. Relative to profit-distributing firms, these organizations are more likely to 'have objectives in line to the contracting agency and be considered more trustworthy, thereby reducing monitoring and enforcement costs associated with opportunism'.[60] They find further that the use of contractors operating under a profit distribution constraint grows with rising complexity in public contracts to mitigate against the impact of contractual incompleteness on transaction costs affecting particularly complex public contracts. In the UK, reported numbers[61] in public service outsourcing convey that trust in awarding contracts to profit-constrained organizations – which would be

---

[59] Hansmann, H.B. (1980) 'The role of nonprofit enterprise', *The Yale Law Journal*, 89(5): 835–901, p 844.

[60] Thornton, J. and Lecy, J. (2019) 'Good enough for government work? An incomplete contracts approach to the use of nonprofits in U.S. federal procurement', *Nonprofit Policy Forum*, 10(3): 1–18, Available from: https://ideas.repec.org/a/bpj/nonpfo/v10y2019i3p18n4.html [Accessed 28 February 2024].

[61] Department for Digital, Culture, Media, and Sport (2022) *The Role of Voluntary, Community, and Social Enterprise (VCSE) Organisations in Public Procurement* [online], August, p 4, Available from: https://assets.publishing.service.gov.uk/government/uploads/system/uploads/attachment_data/file/1100749/The_role_of_Voluntary__Community__and_Social_Enterprises_in_public_procurement.pdf [Accessed 27 February 2024]. See also Tussell (2018) 'New research shows slow growth on awards to social enterprises' [online], 23 July, Available from: www.tussell.com/insights/tussell-social-enterprise-uk-research-shows-slow-growth-on-awards-to-community-interest-companies-cics [Accessed 27 February 2024].

considered VCSE organizations – lags behind (see Chapter Four). A reframing of existing public procurement policy towards sustainable corporate ownership may well help change this.

Similar dynamics affect mutual firms (which may distribute profit to their stakeholder members), indicating a reduction in opportunistic behaviour alongside improved productive capabilities on account of the fact that people 'work harder when they buy into the mission of the organization'.[62] Mutual ownership can, by design, disincentivize a corporate governance model that may exploit key stakeholders. It implies instead 'a commitment by a company to share success with is stakeholders', but also that 'if it is a question of losses, these will not be passed on to stakeholders opportunistically, without regard to the mutual interest'.[63] In the public outsourcing context, the performance of public service mutuals has been tracked in a number of recent publications and reports, citing among the positive impacts of their mutual design both service-related improvements and workforce-related benefits.[64] Productivity of public service

Tussell (2021) *UK Public Procurement through VCSEs, 2016–2020*, Report for the Department for Culture, Media and Sport [online], Available from: https://assets.publishing.service.gov.uk/media/625ecdd7d3bf7 f600d4056a4/UK_Public_Sector_Procurement_through_VCSEs.pdf [Accessed 27 February 2024].

[62] Besley, T. and Ghatak, M. (2003) *Incentives, Choice and Accountability in the Provision of Public Services*, ESRC Centre for Analysis of Risk and Regulation Discussion Paper No 14 [online], p 3, Available from: http:// eprints.lse.ac.uk/36001/1/Disspaper14.pdf [Accessed 28 February 2024]. Michie, J. (2021) 'The impact of mutuality on ownership', in C. Mayer and B. Roche (eds) *Putting Purpose into Practice: The Economics of Mutuality*, Oxford: Oxford University Press, pp 221–230.

[63] Michie, J. (2021) 'The impact of mutuality on ownership', in C. Mayer and B. Roche (eds) *Putting Purpose into Practice: The Economics of Mutuality*, Oxford: Oxford University Press, pp 221–230, p 222.

[64] Social Enterprise UK (2019) *Public Service Mutuals: The State of the Sector* [online], April, Available from: https://assets.publishing.service.gov. uk/media/5ffec084e90e0763a8db979c/Public_Service_Mutuals_-_ The_State_of_the_Sector_2019_V2.pdf [Accessed 28 February 2024].

mutuals between 2012 and 2019 outstripped that of the general public sector, but they also scored higher on quality delivery of care services.[65] Employee ownership in public service mutuals has been linked to 'improving service delivery … with more satisfied users, lower costs and greater productivity in service delivery' alongside the 'intrinsic benefit' of improving employee well-being which has been linked, in turn, to lower levels of absenteeism and staff turnover, higher wages and better retention and recruitment of high-quality staff.[66]

Beyond mutual ownership, growing international attention is more generally given to foundation-owned firms as a hybrid corporate ownership form where a profit-constrained foundation (or trust) holds a controlling share in a profit-distributing company. The foundation is usually compelled in its own corporate charter to continue the business it controls and to reinvest profits into the business, and even to invest some profit in support of a public or charitable cause.[67] Importantly, the foundation corporate body is governed independently of

---

Vickers, I., Lyon, F., Sepulveda, L. and Brennan, G. (2021) *Public Service Mutuals: Transforming How Services are Delivered through Social Enterprise and Democratic Governance?* [online], Centre for Enterprise and Economic Development Research and Middlesex University, in cooperation with Social Enterprise UK, January, Available from: https://assets.publish ing.service.gov.uk/media/630f64978fa8f544842c49b3/Public_Service_ Mutuals_Longitudinal_Case_Study.pdf [Accessed 27 February 2024].

[65] Social Enterprise UK (2019) *Public Service Mutuals: The State of the Sector* [online], April, pp 16–19, Available from https://assets.publishing.service. gov.uk/media/5ffec084e90e0763a8db979c/Public_Service_Mutuals_-_ The_State_of_the_Sector_2019_V2.pdf [Accessed 28 February 2024].

[66] Mutuals Taskforce (2012) 'Mutual and cooperative approaches to delivering local services', written evidence before the House of Commons Communities and Local Government Committee [online], May, Available from: https://publications.parliament.uk/pa/cm201213/cmselect/ cmcomloc/112/112we08.htm [Accessed 27 February 2024].

[67] The recent transfer into foundation ownership of Patagonia, an established multinational commercial firm, for example, includes a commitment to use the company's profits via a dedicated non-profit organization to 'fight the environmental crisis, protect nature and biodiversity, and support

financial investors. It is typically 'under the complete control of a self-appointing board of directors whose compensation is completely divorced from the profitability of the company and who cannot be replaced by anyone except themselves' and who are therefore in effect 'impervious to shareholder votes and hostile acquisitions'.[68] From the perspective of classical agency analysis in corporate governance, which assumes that alignment of financial incentives of company directors and shareholders improves a firm's outcomes, the profitability of many foundation–owned firms presents an anomaly. It implies, Hansmann and Thomsen conclude, that 'corporate directors do not necessarily require a monetary stake to become effective corporate overseers. Rather, an appropriately designed governance structure, working through nonpecuniary incentives, can perhaps perform effectively not just in limited circumstances, but in a broad range of industries.'[69] In the UK, foundation–owned firms are less popular than elsewhere in Europe, a discrepancy that has been explained by a range of factors, including the differences in the UK trust structure, less attractive tax incentives and more simply a 'lack of awareness amongst corporation owners of this option'.[70] But several

thriving communities' – Chouinard, Y. (undated) 'What is the Holdfast Collective and what does it do?' in 'Earth is now our only shareholder', *Patagonia* [online], Available from: https://eu.patagonia.com/gb/en/ownership/ [Accessed 28 February 2024].

[68] Hansmann, H. and Thomsen, S. (2021) 'The governance of foundation-owned firms', *Journal of Legal Analysis*, 13(1): 172–230, p 173.

[69] Hansmann, H. and Thomsen, S. (2021) 'The governance of foundation-owned firms', *Journal of Legal Analysis*, 13(1): 172–230, p 225. See further Kristensen, P.H. and Morgan, G. (2018) 'Danish foundations and cooperatives as forms of corporate governance: origins and impacts on firm strategies and societies', in N. Boeger and C. Villiers (eds) *Shaping the Corporate Landscape: Between Corporate Reform and Enterprise Diversity*, Oxford: Hart Publishing, pp 271 – 288.

[70] Prism (2021) 'The foundation-owned companies model: UK vs abroad' [online], 18 March, Available from: https://prismthegiftfund.co.uk/latest/foundation-owned-companies/ [Accessed 28 February 2024].

trust-owned companies do now exist in the UK, and this model has also been further developed in UK-based academic work.[71] In the context of public service outsourcing, foundation ownership has potentially important governance advantages over commercially owned corporate providers in terms of reducing risks of opportunistic behaviour and financialization (discussed further in Chapter Six).

Box 5.3

That profits can be allocated in different ways in the social economy is illustrated by the legal forms of cooperative society and community benefit society in the UK. Both are corporate bodies registered under the same legislation and regulated by the Financial Conduct Authority (FCA).[a] They are set up to conduct trade either for the interest of their members, in the case of a cooperative society, or for the wider benefit of the community, in the case of the community benefit society. Both formats offer their members the benefit of limited liability and an organization with separate legal personality, but governed by a management committee and subject to the principle of 'one member, one vote' to enable democratic control. Cooperative societies can distribute a share of their profit to members, determined typically by the level of a member's transactions with the society. However, the FCA clarifies that if profit distribution is considered 'the main purpose or "object" of the society's actual or intended business, then it does not meet the definition of a co-operative society'.[b] Unlike a cooperative society, any profit made by a community benefit society

---

Bottge, D. (2021) 'The foundation-owned company model: the path to build tomorrow's society by unifying long-termism and philanthropic impact', *Philanthropy Impact*, 24: 12–14, Available from: www.philanthropy-impact.org/sites/default/files/pdf/philanthropy-impact-magazine-issue-24-p4_0.pdf [Accessed 28 February 2024].

[71] Mayer, C. (2014) *Firm Commitment: Why the Corporation Is Failing us and How to Restore Trust in It*, Oxford: Oxford University Press. See also, for discussion of a variety of formats, Purpose Foundation, *Steward Ownership: Rethinking Ownership in the 21st Century* [online], Available from: https://purpose-economy.org/content/uploads/purposebooklet_en.pdf [Accessed 28 February 2024].

must be used to benefit the community; either by reinvesting it into the society's business or by funding, for example, charitable activities for community benefit.[c] Community benefit societies must also use their assets to benefit the community. The legislation makes available statutory entrenched wording for an asset lock provision they may incorporate into their rules. Cooperative societies may still adopt a voluntary asset lock provision.[d]

a   Cooperative and Community Benefit Societies Act 2014.
b   Financial Conduct Authority (2024), Registration Function under the Cooperative and Community Benefit Societies Act 2014 Guide, Release 36, May, Section 4.2.1, Available from: https://www.handbook.fca.org.uk/handbook/RFCCBS.pdf [Accessed 17 May 2024].
c   Financial Conduct Authority (2024), Registration Function under the Cooperative and Community Benefit Societies Act 2014 Guide, Release 36, May, Section 5.1.9, Available from: https://www.handbook.fca.org.uk/handbook/RFCCBS.pdf [Accessed 17 May 2024].
d   Community Benefit Societies (Restriction on Use of Assets) Regulations 2006. See also Financial Conduct Authority (2024), Registration Function under the Cooperative and Community Benefit Societies Act 2014 Guide, Release 36, May, Sections 3.4.12–3.4.16 ('Statutory asset locks') and 5.1.12–5.1.14 ('Use of assets'), Available from: https://www.handbook.fca.org.uk/handbook/RFCCBS.pdf [Accessed 17 May 2024].

SIX

Nurturing Sustainable Ownership

Reversing financialization

The state may seek to reverse financialization[1] in the corporate economy by awarding more public contracts to private providers in sustainable ownership. In this way, it may address an important secondary purpose of nurturing a less financialized corporate governance model and more sustainable design of corporate ownership in the wider economy while, at the same time, improving the outsourcing of public services – aspiring to create win-win. Initially at least, providers in sustainable ownership may rely on the largesse of the state by receiving payment for public service delivery as a form of nurturing, so that by delivering public contracts, they expand their capacity to operate as economically independent firms. This may, in the case of small firms or startups, act as a form of incubation to help them grow initial capacity to become established and eventually able to deliver not just more public contracts but also private contracts. In the case of larger and already established firms in sustainable ownership, it may nurture their continued capitalization and growth. We see the potential for a positive feedback loop between improving public service outsourcing

---

[1] Borrowed from Deakin, S. (2018) 'Reversing financialization: shareholder value and the legal reform of corporate governance', in C. Driver and G. Thompson (eds) *Corporate Governance in Contention*, Oxford: Oxford University Press, pp 25–41.

and diversifying the wider economy by introducing more sustainable corporate ownership designs.[2] The government's current procurement policies addressing VCSE organizations and SMEs already recognize some of these win–win opportunities (see Chapter One), highlighting that governance in these organizations can help deliver 'smarter, more thoughtful and effective public services [while also rendering] the economy more innovative, resilient and productive'.[3] A reframing of the existing policies could further strengthen and expand this by encouraging contracting authorities to favour a wider range of sustainable corporate forms (see Chapter Five) to deliver a wider range of public services.

Financialized corporate governance creates problems in the wider economy and for society that reach far beyond the delivery of public services.[4] Unlike in past economic crises, the economic issue since the global financial crisis in 2008 is less about mass unemployment and more to do with the fact that many in employment remain poor, their wages stagnating as those who own capital extract an increasing share of the economy.[5] These inequalities are exacerbated where investors

2 Boeger, N. (2018) 'Public procurement and business for value: looking for alignment in law and practice', in A. Sanchez-Graells (ed) *Smart Public Procurement and Labour Standards: Pushing the Discussion after RegioPost*, Oxford: Hart Publishing, pp 115–139. Barraket, J., Keast, R. and Furneaux, C. (2015) *Social Procurement and New Public Governance*, Abingdon: Routledge.

3 Department for Digital, Culture, Media, and Sport (2022) *The Role of Voluntary, Community, and Social Enterprise (VCSE) Organisations in Public Procurement* [online], August, p 3 (Foreword by the VCSE Crown Representative), Available from: https://assets.publishing.service.gov. uk/government/uploads/system/uploads/attachment_data/file/1100 749/The_role_of_Voluntary__Community__and_Social_Enterprises_ in_public_procurement.pdf [Accessed 27 February 2024].

4 Christophers, B. (2020) *Rentier Capitalism: Who Owns the Economy and Who Pays for It?* London: Verso.

5 Piketty, T. (2014) *Capital in the Twenty-First Century*, Cambridge, MA: Harvard University Press.

are able to extract a growing share of a company's profit in the pursuit of shareholder value but profits are not shared with the workers who contribute to their generation.[6] In financialized firms, resilience and sustainability are deprioritized. The focus rests instead on generating return on investment, even if the company ends up operating as a 'zombie'.[7] As shareholders are prioritized, accountability for the social impact and environmental externalities of corporate activities, on the other hand, is sidelined, unless mandated by regulatory norms, which can be hard to design and even harder to enforce in a globalized economic context of regulatory competition. At its worst, this generates levels of corporate recklessness and irresponsibility, reflected in the largest recent corporate governance scandals, from Enron to BP Horizon to Volkswagen, among others.[8] As financialized firms set out to minimize exposure to regulatory norms and aggressively pursue tax efficiencies, they also create additional cost for the state. A governance gap, similar to that affecting the contractual relationship in public service outsourcing, impacts on the government's role as regulatory authority over financialized companies: their internal corporate governance exacerbates the potential for formalized conflict between the regulated business organization and the regulating authority, as public and private interests are widely misaligned. And the more extreme the misalignment, the harder each

---

[6]   Stout, L. (2012) 'How shareholder primacy gets the empirical evidence wrong', in *The Shareholder Value Myth: How Putting Shareholders First Harms Investors, Corporations and the Public*, Oakland, CA: Berrett-Koehler, pp 47–60.

[7]   Urionabarrenetxea, S., Domingo Garcia-Merino, J., San-Jose, L. and Retolaza, J.L. (2018) 'Living with zombie companies: do we know where the threat lies?', *European Management Journal*, 36(3): 408–420.

[8]   Ireland, P. (2018) 'Corporate schizophrenia: the institutional origins of corporate irresponsibility', in N. Boeger and C. Villiers (eds) *Shaping the Corporate Landscape: Between Corporate Reform and Enterprise Diversity*, Oxford: Hart Publishing, pp 13 – 39.

side will pull in the pursuit of its interest – the stronger the company drives to prioritize its shareholders, the stronger the state must step in by imposing regulatory constraints to protect a public interest. In this tug of war, the state can expect to have to expend additional public resource to impose effective regulatory accountability on financialized firms that otherwise would continue to prioritize narrow corporate goals, mainly to protect capital investors.[9]

By awarding public contracts repeatedly to companies operating in financialized governance, the state in effect supports their extractive corporate model by making available important public funding that allows them to sustain this design, grow their business and consolidate their market position. In doing so, the state not only sustains a mode of public contracting that requires it to tightly control these providers (see Chapters Two and Three), but supports their corporate ownership design and mode of corporate governance, affirming it by selecting them as private contracting partners or even strategic suppliers. It signals in effect that the prioritizing of financial investors above other interests in extractive corporate design is politically acceptable, even if it reduces the share of wealth for other stakeholders in the economy and creates additional costs (including indirect and opportunity costs) elsewhere for the state.

The legal design of organizations in sustainable corporate ownership – with reconfigured internal rules on purpose, power and profit, as set out in Chapter Five – means their ability to prioritize capital is tempered, rendering them less vulnerable to the levels of financialization that create problems for society. The ambition is for workers to capture a larger share of the surpluses they produce, for the role and interests of stakeholders to be given more room within the governance of the firm and,

---

[9]   Wilks, S. (2013) *The Political Power of the Business Corporation*, Cheltenham: Edward Elgar.

overall, for the creation of a more resilient long-term economy and a better regulatory partnership between these firms and the state. While the designs of organizations in sustainable corporate ownership are diverse (as discussed in Chapter Five), these reconfigurations all have the effect, and often the distinct intention, of avoiding the sort of economic organizing we see in financialized firms and, more widely, of integrating sustainability as an alternative governance principle – a 'counter-story' to the narrow commercial commitment to prioritizing profit – into the wider corporate economy.[10] Some might describe this as an accountable form of capitalism where companies balance their responsibilities towards any financial investors against those they owe to wider stakeholders, society and the environment;[11] others may see it, more simply, as a kinder version of capitalism[12] or a more democratic economy.[13]

The variation of individual corporate designs illustrates how this may be possible. For example, effective co-determination on the company board of a commercial company, by incorporating a significant number of directors who are appointed directly by the workforce, alters the company's

[10] Boeger, N. (2020) 'Sustainable corporate governance: trimming or sowing?', in M. Pieraccini and T. Novitz (eds) *Legal Perspectives on Sustainability*, Bristol: Policy Press, pp 101–123, p 103.

[11] See, in the US, the proposal for an Accountable Capitalism Act by Senator Elizabeth Warren, Available from: www.warren.senate.gov/imo/media/doc/Accountable%20Capitalism%20Act%20One-Pager.pdf [Accessed 27 February 2024].

[12] Thomas, D., Dempsey, J. and Hooker, L. (2023) 'John Lewis will always be owned by staff, says boss', *BBC News* [online], 10 May, Available from: www.bbc.co.uk/news/business-65520696 [Accessed 28 February 2024]. Storey, J. and Salaman, G. (2017) 'Employee ownership and the drive to do business responsibly: a study of the John Lewis Partnership', *Oxford Review of Economic Policy*, 33(2): 339–354, p 341.

[13] Kelly, M. and Howard, T. (2019) *The Making of a Democratic Economy: How to Build Prosperity for the Many, Not the Few*, Oakland: Berrett-Koehler.

governance design to temper financialization because control rights are reorganized.[14] Positive effects, including improved pay and working conditions, investment in training and skills, and better corporate decision making and productivity, have been reported.[15] A transfer into employee ownership, likewise, has been linked to tempering corporate financialization by reducing financial risk and conflicts between shareholders and employees while 'encouraging employees to work hard, strengthening team cooperation and increasing the supervision of executives'.[16] John Lewis Partnership, for example, has an expectation of a 'Partner–Customer–Profit cycle', relying on member partners' personal investment in the company to improve resilience and performance.[17] Mutually owned firms have generally been identified as more resilient, due to different levels of risk-taking, than firms where profits are distributed to investors.[18] Mutual ownership design, because membership

---

[14] Deakin, S. (2018) 'Reversing financialization: shareholder value and the legal reform of corporate governance', in C. Driver and G. Thompson (eds) *Corporate Governance in Contention*, Oxford: Oxford University Press, pp 25–41.

[15] High Pay Centre (2022) *Worker Voice in Corporate Governance: How to Bring Perspectives from the Workforce into the Boardroom* [online], October, Available from: https://highpaycentre.org/wp-content/uploads/2022/11/STA0922916658-001_aFFT-Pay-Ratios-Report_1022_v5.pdf [Accessed 28 February 2024].

[16] Feng, Y., Yu, Q., Nan, X. and Cai, Y. (2022) 'Can employee stock ownership plans reduce corporate financialization? Evidence from China', *Economic Analysis and Policy*, 73: 140–151, p 142. See also Tran, P.H.H. (2021) 'Does employee stock ownership program reduce a company's stock volatility during the Covid-19 lockdown?', *Journal of Behavioral and Experimental Finance*, 32: 100558. doi: 10.1016/j.jbef.2021.100558

[17] Storey, J. and Salaman, G. (2017) 'Employee ownership and the drive to do business responsibly: a study of the John Lewis Partnership', *Oxford Review of Economic Policy*, 33(2): 339–354, p 340.

[18] Billiet, A., Dufays, F., Friedel, S. and Staessens, M. (2021) 'The resilience of the cooperative model: how do cooperatives deal with the COVID-19 crisis?', *Strategic Change*, 30: 99–108. International Cooperative and Mutual Insurance Federation (2023) *Global Mutual Market Share 2023*

is vested in key stakeholders, means managers retain greater flexibility to balance financial against social and environmental factors in their decision making. Data indicate that mutual organizations are more open to selecting economic partners (including suppliers, consumers and employees) on the basis of socially relevant criteria, including selection of a more diverse workforce or customers who may be considered higher risk or seen as presenting more complex needs.[19] Also, they tend to perform highly on employee satisfaction and workforce motivation, and this generally has a positive impact on their

[online], June, Available from: www.icmif.org/wp-content/uploads/2023/06/ICMIF-Global-Mutual-Market-Share-2023.pdf [Accessed 9 March 2024]. Sheperd, J. (2023) *Mutual Understanding: The Modern Mutual Sector and How to Support It* [online], Social Market Foundation, June, p 23, Available from: www.smf.co.uk/wp-content/uploads/2023/06/Mutual-understanding-June-2023.pdf [Accessed 28 February 2024]. Gherken, C. (2021) 'Adaptability and resilience in the mutuals sector – speech by Charlotte Gherken' [online], 4 October, Available from: www.bankofengland.co.uk/speech/2021/october/charlotte-gerken-speech-at-the-association-of-financial-mutuals-conference#:~:text=We%20have%20seen%20the%20mutual,and%20payment%20holidays%2C%20where%20appropriate [Accessed 28 February 2024]. Business Council of Co-operatives and Mutuals and Mutuo (2020) *Leading the Resilience: Cooperative and Mutual Business through COVID-19* [online], Available from: https://bccm.coop/wp-content/uploads/2020/11/BCCM-Leading-Resilience-Report.pdf [Accessed 28 February 2024].

[19] Business Council of Co-operatives and Mutuals (2022) *Gender Diversity among Chairs and Chief Executives of the Top 100 Co-Operative and Mutual Enterprises (2016–2022)* [online], June, Available from: https://bccm.coop/wp-content/uploads/2023/03/BCCM-Gender-Diversity-Report-June2022.pdf [Accessed 28 February 2024]. Maunder, S. (2019) 'Banks vs building societies: where can you get the best mortgage rate?', *Which?* [online], 31 May, Available from: www.which.co.uk/news/article/banks-vs-building-societies-where-can-you-get-the-best-mortgage-rate-aQPI06u6I0ak [Accessed 28 February 2024]. Cavaglieri, C. (2021) 'Banks failing to support disabled customers', *Which?* [online], 27 July, Available from: www.which.co.uk/news/article/banks-failing-to-support-disabled-customers-aROeo1O9ayfc [Accessed 28 February 2024].

productivity,[20] as long as employee participation in decision making is effective and supportive human resources policies are in place.[21] John Lewis Partnership and Nationwide Building Society – two of the largest UK mutually owned firms – were among the top ten organizations for customer satisfaction in the UK in 2023.[22]

Firms operating under a profit distribution constraint exist not only in the social economy – where this feature is typical – but also in the wider economy (as we saw in Chapter Five), for example in foundation-owned companies that lock in their capital for reinvestment or to support the shareholding foundation. Much like social economy organizations, but without the distinct orientation to operate as such, their operating model constitutes a form of 'steward ownership' that prioritizes a productive purpose over profit and vests control rights only in people actively engaged or connected to the organization, rather than in external investors. Thus defined, steward–owned firms as a distinct form of sustainable corporate design commit that: the profits they generate are either reinvested into the business, used to cover capital costs or donated to charity; and voting shares can only be held by stewards – that is, people in or close to the business.[23]

---

[20] Michie, J. (2021) 'The impact of mutuality on ownership', in C. Mayer and B. Roche (eds) *Putting Purpose into Practice: The Economics of Mutuality*, Oxford: Oxford University Press, pp 221–30.

[21] Basterretxea, I. and Storey, J. (2018), 'Do employee-owned firms produce more positive employee behavioural outcomes? If not why not? A British-Spanish comparative analysis', *British Journal of Industrial Relations* 56(2): 292–319

[22] Institute of Customer Service (2023) *UK Customer Satisfaction Index* [online], July, Available from: https://lp.instituteofcustomerservice. com/hubfs/ICS%20UKCSI%20Main_Report_July_2023_ONLINE. pdf [Accessed 28 February 2024].

[23] Purpose Foundation (undated) *Steward-Ownership: Rethinking Ownership in the 21st Century* [online], p 11, Available from: https://purpose-economy.org/content/uploads/purposebooklet_en.pdf [Accessed 28 February 2024].

In Germany, political discussion over a proposed statutory 'company in bound capital' – a tailored corporate form that would lock in steward ownership without the need for a foundation-owned corporate structure – has exposed both demand for these steward-owned firms in promoting socially responsible entrepreneurship and concrete governance concerns in relation to a new preconfigured form.[24] These concrete debates are challenging details in the design of sustainable corporate ownership, but underline its general importance in tempering financialized corporate governance models in the wider economy.[25]

Legislative debates in Europe have also advanced the development of purpose-driven legal designs for firms operating in the wider economy.[26] Unlike for social enterprises that are dedicated to a specific community purpose and whose assets and capital are fully or partially locked to avoid distribution or mission drift (see the discussion of community interest companies in Chapter Five), the ambition of these new corporate forms is to transition to a sustainable corporate governance model by introducing a purposeful design into commercially operating firms that continue to distribute profit

---

[24] Wissenschaftlicher Beirat beim Bundesministerium für Finanzen (2022) *Zum Vorschlag für eine GmbH mit gebundenem Vermögen*, Stellungnahme 04/22 [online], Available from: www.bundesfinanzministerium.de/Content/DE/Downloads/Ministerium/Wissenschaftlicher-Beirat/Gutachten/gmbh-mit-gebundenem-vermoegen.pdf?__blob=publicationFile&v=2 [Accessed 9 March 2024].

[25] See also Hansmann and Thomsen's conclusion that foundation-owned companies 'merit greater attention in today's widespread search for more socially responsible forms of enterprise' – Hansmann, H. and Thomsen, S. (2021) 'The governance of foundation-owned firms', *Journal of Legal Analysis*, 13(1): 172–230, p 225.

[26] Levillain, K. and Segrestin, B. (2019) 'From primacy to purpose commitment: how emerging profit-with-purpose corporations open new corporate governance avenues', *European Management Journal*, 37(5): 637–647.

to their investors to ensure their capitalization but still temper financialization. A purpose-driven company may integrate into its constitution any lawful corporate objective representing a productive purpose that will then guide its activities. In addition, it may also specify the 'conditions under which it considers these activities can be responsible and sustainable'.[27] In Chapter Five, we saw the use of B Corp certification and the US benefit corporation – both of which have been internationalized – to create purpose-driven companies.[28] A separate example of the trend to create new purpose-driven corporate legal forms is the French 'société à mission', introduced in 2019 under the PACTE (Le Plan d'Action pour la Croissance et la Transformation des Entreprises) law.[29] Under this law, a French company wishing to incorporate as a société à mission can do so by defining a raison d'être in its constitution as well as setting out constitutional objectives that address social and environmental issues, to guide its corporate activities in the pursuit of its raison d'être. Concrete governance changes are also required, including the setting up of a mission committee, independent of the board of directors, with powers to investigate and monitor the company's mission as well as an external governance process to regularly audit the implementation of its mission. Many medium-sized but also a number of large French companies, even some listed

---

[27] Segrestin, B. and Levillain, K. (2023) 'Profit-with-purpose corporations: why purpose needs law and why it matters for management', *European Management Review*, 20(4): 733–740, p 735.

[28] See, for example, Stubbs, W. (2017) 'Characterising B Corps as a sustainable business model: an exploratory study of B Corps in Australia', *Journal of Cleaner Production*, 144: 299–312. Ventura, L. (2023) 'Social enterprises and benefit corporations in Italy', in H. Peter, C. Vargas Vasserot, J. Alcalde Silva (eds) *The International Handbook of Social Enterprise Law*, Berlin: Springer, pp 651–674.

[29] Loi no 2019–486 du 22 mai 2019 relative à la croissance et la transformation des entreprises, Available from: www.economie.gouv.fr/loi-pacte-croissance-transformation-entreprises [Accessed 11 March 2024].

companies, have chosen to incorporate as a société à mission. The form clearly is focused on combining profit and purpose rather than creating social enterprises which impose profit distribution constraints or limit the firm to exercising social activities. Incorporating as société à mission 'does not equate to forgoing profits. It means that the company's purpose incorporates additional ambitions', tempering the adverse impact that financialized corporate governance and the prioritizing of profit might otherwise have on society.[30]

There are important links between these purpose-driven corporate ownership designs, and other variations of sustainable corporate ownership, to wider discussions over the future role of corporate business organizations, and of corporate law and governance, in our national and global economies and for our societies. That role, many now argue, should *by default* (not by choice, as in the examples provided) be to 'produce profitable solutions for the problems of people and planet [...] not to produce profits *per se*, nor to profit from producing problems for people and planet'.[31] All corporate organizations should, in other words, expect to embrace in their corporate ownership and governance design sustainability and social value as primary concerns, understood in terms of social, environmental and economic objectives.[32] This in turn would require important changes to existing national and international corporate legal

---

[30] Segrestin, B. and Levillain, K. (2023) 'Profit-with-purpose corporations: why purpose needs law and why it matters for management', *European Management Review*, 20(4): 733–740, p 735.

[31] The British Academy (2018) *Reforming Business for the 21st Century: A Framework for the Future of the Corporation* [online], p 24 (italics in original), Available from: www.thebritishacademy.ac.uk/documents/76/Reform ing-Business-for-21st-Century-British-Academy.pdf [Accessed 11 March 2024].

[32] Boeger, N. (2021) *Amending UK Company Law for a Regenerative Economy* [online], Institute of Directors, Available from: https://betterbusinessact. org/wp-content/uploads/2021/05/IoD-CG-Centre-Amending-UK-Company-Law.pdf [Accessed 27 February 2024]. Social Enterprise UK (2023) *The Social Value Roadmap 2032* [online], June, p 21, Available

and governance frameworks which are currently not designed to encourage or enforce this but could, if redesigned, act as important levers for *system change* to the way in which corporations operate. This could be done by reconfiguring rules on purpose, power and profit, creating sustainable ownership design by default rather than as a matter of individual choice.[33] It would still maintain different variations of sustainable ownership (for example, there would be a distinction between social enterprises, mutually owned legal design and investor-owned legal design), but all of the choices available would align with economic, social and environmental aspects of sustainability. Concretely, such as system change would potentially require the redrafting of important existing default rules in corporate law and governance, including on corporate purpose and fiduciary duties, on board membership and corporate committees, on executive pay, on enforcement and regulatory oversight, and on auditing, accounting, reporting and (potentially) disclosure requirements, extending existing obligations further to measure and account for performance related to sustainability and social value.[34]

Such wide-ranging changes to the legal and governance framework for corporations could only be developed

---

from: www.socialenterprise.org.uk/seuk-report/the-social-value-road map/ [Accessed 11 March 2024].

[33] Mayer, C. (2023) 'Shareholderism versus stakeholderism—a misconceived contradiction', *Cornell Law Review*, 106(7): 1859–1879.

[34] Boeger, N. (2021) *Amending UK Company Law for a Regenerative Economy* [online], Institute of Directors, Available from: https://betterbusinessact. org/wp-content/uploads/2021/05/IoD-CG-Centre-Amending-UK-Company-Law.pdf [Accessed 27 February 2024]. Social Enterprise UK (2023) *The Social Value Roadmap 2032* [online], June, p 15, Available from: www.socialenterprise.org.uk/seuk-report/the-social-value-road map/ [Accessed 11 March 2024]. The British Academy (2021) *Policy & Practice for Purposeful Business: The Final Report of the Future of the Corporation Programme* [online], p 20, Available from: www.thebritish academy.ac.uk/publications/policy-and-practice-for-purposeful-busin ess/ [Accessed 11 March 2024]. Segrestin, B. and Levillain, K. (2023)

incrementally. Meanwhile, however, experimentation that relies on sustainable corporate design by choice, as voluntary adjustment of corporate legal form by reconfiguring rules on purpose, power and profit inside the organization, plays a complementary role.[35] In all its variations, such experimentation has the important impact to strengthen sustainability in our wider economies and avoid the negative consequences of financialized corporate capitalism. It raises the possibility that as more and more firms choose sustainable designs, legislators and regulators as well as markets will, despite the downward pressure of regulatory and market competition in a globalized economic context, come to *expect* these designs of companies as a default. But in practice, while there is no shortage of proposals nationally and internationally for how a transformed law and governance framework might impose aspects of sustainable corporate design by default, these are still politically rather difficult choices to take.[36] In this difficult political context, a public outsourcing policy that supports private suppliers in sustainable ownership would provide an important additional governance instrument

---

'Profit-with-purpose corporations: why purpose needs law and why it matters for management', *European Management Review*, 20(4): 733–740, p 736. See also the EU Corporate Sustainability Reporting Directive (Directive 2022/2464), Available from: https://eur-lex.eur opa.eu/legal-content/EN/TXT/?uri=CELEX:32022L2464 [Accessed 11 March 2024]. On disclosure, see the duty of vigilance imposed on corporations by France's PACTE law, discussed by Segrestin, B. and Levillain, K. (2023) 'Profit-with-purpose corporations: why purpose needs law and why it matters for management', *European Management Review*, 20(4): 733–740, p 734.

[35] See, for example, Ferrarini, G. and Zhu, S. (2021) *Is there a Role for Benefit Corporations in the New Sustainable Governance Framework?* European Corporate Governance Institute Working Paper No 588/2021 [online], June, Available from: www.ecgi.global/sites/default/files/working_pap ers/documents/ferrarinizhufinal.pdf [Accessed 11 March 2024].

[36] See, for example, the EU sustainable corporate governance framework proposed in 2020 following a report by Ernst and Young for the European Commission – Ernst and Young (2020) *Study on Directors' Duties and*

for the state to accelerate, via public contracting, the development of more sustainable corporate designs.

The need to nurture

From a practical perspective, firms in sustainable ownership currently face various tangible, widespread and sometimes complex, barriers to economic success which a supportive outsourcing policy might help them address – including existing barriers in getting their enterprise off the ground, in accessing suitable financial capital or growing and scaling their business in markets that are often dominated by large commercial corporations. For some of these firms, their slower growth is linked directly to differences from other commercial firms in their approach to risk-taking. Foundation-owned firms, for example, have been found to avoid risks associated with extreme sales growth, aiming instead for a conservative growth strategy.[37] But independent of these factors, for many the struggle to access suitable finance is a practical concern, as routes to raising capital from traditional equity investors will be restricted as a consequence of their legal design and the continuing scepticism among those investors towards sustainable corporate forms.[38]

Sustainable Corporate Governance [online], July, Available from: https://op.europa.eu/en/publication-detail/-/publication/e47928a2-d20b-11ea-adf7-01aa75ed71a1/language-en [Accessed 12 March 2024]. The proposed framework has, meanwhile, been reduced. See the proposal for an EU Directive on Corporate Sustainability Due Diligence, dated 23 February 2022, Available from: https://commission.europa.eu/business-economy-euro/doing-business-eu/corporate-sustainability-due-diligence_en [Accessed 12 March 2024].

[37] Block, J. and Fathollahi, R. (2023) 'Foundation ownership and firm growth', *Review of Managerial Science*, 17: 2633–2654.

[38] See Achleitner, A.K., Bazhutov, D., Betzer, A., Block, J. and Hosseini, F. (2020) 'Foundation ownership and shareholder value: an event study', *Review of Managerial Science*, 14(3): 459–484.

Skeptical investors tend to prioritize a shareholder value mindset and arguments that stress effectiveness and legitimacy in shareholder-centric governance, and are therefore relatively protective of the status quo.[39] Profit-driven investors simply do not believe that a sustainable corporate form will make them enough money in the short term or even in the long term. As one commentator put it in 2017, 'public-market B Corps are rare because investors hate them' – though B Corps had, in fact, by then attracted considerable investment.[40] Other forms – for example, many mutually owned firms – are simply not designed to accommodate external equity investment unless they are prepared to fully or partially demutualize; but the alternatives, including debt funding, member contributions and retained earnings, may not take them far enough in scaling their business.[41] Similarly, for many social enterprises

---

[39] See, for example, Investor Forum and London Business School (2022) *What Does Stakeholder Capitalism Mean for Investors?* [online], January, Available from: www.investorforum.org.uk/wp-content/uploads/securepdfs/2022/01/Stakeholder-Capitalism_Report.pdf [Accessed 12 March 2024]. For a recent academic argument against 'stakeholderism', see Bebchuk, L.A. and Tallarita, R. (2020) 'The illusory promise of stakeholder governance', *Cornell Law Review*, 106(1): 91–178, and a response in Mayer, C. (2023) 'Shareholderism versus stakeholderism—a misconceived contradiction', *Cornell Law Review*, 106(7): 1859–1879.

[40] Chafkin, M. and Cao, J. (2017) 'The barbarians are at Etsy's hand-hewn, responsibly sourced gates', *Bloomberg* [online], 18 May, Available from: www.bloomberg.com/news/features/2017-05-18/the-barbarians-are-at-etsy-s-hand-hewn-responsibly-sourced-gates?embedded-check out=true [Accessed 12 March 2024]. See the response by The Shareholder Commons (2017) 'How investors really feel about B Corps', *B the Change* [online], 25 May, Available from: https://bthechange.com/how-invest ors-really-feel-about-b-corps-7dcf7988a6e3 [Accessed 12 March 2024].

[41] Sheperd, J. (2023) *Mutual Understanding: The Modern Mutual Sector and How to Support It* [online], Social Market Foundation, June, p 8, Available from: www.smf.co.uk/wp-content/uploads/2023/06/Mutual-unders tanding-June-2023.pdf [Accessed 28 February 2024].

and purpose-driven firms, investment design is a matter essentially of creating sufficient trust between the investor and the company:

> Entrepreneurs have to worry about investor commitment, lest they push them to marginalize their social goals for financial gains. Impact investors want to invest their dollars for social good but will have trouble monitoring the social value being generated. Unless both parties are willing to trust each other, investment will be limited and capital-constrained benefit corporations will be limited in the social value they can create.[42]

Against these challenges, the question of sustainable investment is increasingly being raised not so much as a normative issue but in practical terms, framed as a matter of innovative and sustainable financial design with a focus on aligning investment opportunities and sustainable corporate legal forms. A variety of investment instruments are being developed in the UK and elsewhere to enable these goals. They incorporate debt and equity financing options, including possibilities to raise permanent share capital in mutual or cooperative forms.[43] They also include tailored equity crowdfunding solutions.[44]

---

[42] Brakman Reiser, D. and Dean, S.A. (2017) 'Financing the benefit corporation', *Seattle University Law Review*, 40: 793–819, p 818, Available from: https://scholarship.law.bu.edu/faculty_scholarship/3413 [Accessed 28 February 2024].

[43] Michael Andrews, A. (2015) *Survey of Cooperative Capital* [online], International Cooperative Alliance, 6 March, Available from: https://ica.coop/sites/default/files/2021-11/ICA%20survey%20of%20co-operative%20capital%20report%20EN.pdf [Accessed 7 March 2024]. Co-Operatives (Permanent Shares), volume 730, debated on Wednesday 29 March 2023, Available from: https://hansard.parliament.uk/commons/2023-03-29/debates/DDD4BAEC-F812-4A42-90C9-8BB83DA51049/Co-Operatives(PermanentShares) [Accessed 12 March 2024].

[44] Heminway, J. (2017) *Financing Social Enterprise: Is the Crowd the Answer?* University of Tennessee Legal Studies Research Paper No 327 [online],

And of course there is a role for different types of social or impact investment funding options.[45] These all represent a growing effort to match individual financial needs of various sustainable corporate forms with the equally diverse expectations of individual investors or funds. But where traditional investment is unavailable, these financing solutions, often involving a blend of debt and equity instruments, will be non-standardized and often expensive to design.[46] Tax incentives can provide further support but often do not compensate for wider access to finance.[47] Unless and until

---

Available from SSRN: https://ssrn.com/abstract=2997262 [Accessed 12 March 2024].

[45] Lyon, F. and Owen, R. (2019) 'Financing social enterprises and the demand for social investment', *Strategic Change*, 28(1): 47–57. Boeger, N. (2024) 'Social enterprise in the United Kingdom', in D. Brakman Reiser, S.A. Dean and G. Lideikyte Huber (eds) *Social Enterprise Law: A Multijurisdictional Comparative Review*, Cambridge: Intersentia, pp 577 - 603. Note that for public service mutuals, access to finance has been found to be a 'relatively infrequent' barrier; see Social Enterprise UK (2019) *Public Service Mutuals: The State of the Sector* [online], April, p 19, Available from https://assets.publishing.service.gov.uk/media/5ffec084e 90e0763a8db979c/Public_Service_Mutuals_-_The_State_of_the_Sec tor_2019_V2.pdf [Accessed 28 February 2024].

[46] Brakman Reiser, D. and Dean, S.A. (2017) *Social Enterprise Law: Trust, Public Benefit and Capital Markets*, Oxford: Oxford University Press. In relation to UK employee ownership finance, see Hall, E. and Gorman, D. (2020) *Capital Partners? Why It's Time for Finance and Employee Ownership to Talk* [online], Ownership at Work, Available from: https://baxendaleow nership.co.uk/wp-content/uploads/2020/04/Ownership-at-Work-Capi tal-Partners.pdf [Accessed 13 March 2024].

[47] For example, although current UK government support for the employee ownership trust mitigates at least some of the traditional barriers to financing in employee ownership, it does so only partially, at the point of an initial transfer of shares. The scheme currently allows for deferred consideration to finance the initial transfer of shares to employees when the original owner leaves the firm, often because they wish to retire. See Pendleton, A., Robinson, A. and Nuttall, G. (2023) 'Employee ownership in the UK', *Journal of Participation and Employee Ownership*, 6(3): 194–214.

finance is being repurposed[48] to support sustainable corporate forms, these forms are not going to have the same access to investment and finance as fully commercial corporations.

Connecting up public procurement policies and the development of sustainable corporate ownership forms provides a link in this wider context which has, perhaps strangely, been neglected so far, at least insofar as the development of concrete policy proposals goes. Corporate initiatives to support sustainable corporate design tend to emphasize the need generally for developing a purposeful partnership between state and business. A recent large research project on the 'future of the corporation' stresses that it is precisely in areas 'where corporations perform important public and social functions, that private and public purposes need to be aligned through the adoption of public purposes in corporate charters and articles of association'.[49] The contracting partnership in public service outsourcing is of course a point in hand (but the project did not explore this in detail). The state, on the other hand, has, as discussed in earlier chapters, intensified its focus on procuring sustainably, and in the UK, this is generally framed as the intention to secure wider social value for economic, environmental and social well-being by requiring private suppliers to incorporate social value into their delivery of public services (see Chapters One and Seven). But its policies remain narrow in their framing of the type of corporate ownership designs that may have aspects of social value, or sustainability,

---

[48] Pitt-Watson, D. and Mann, H. (2022) 'The purposeful corporation and the role of the finance industry', *Journal of the British Academy*, 10(s5): 125–161. Bone Dodds, G. (2020) *Barriers to Growing the Purpose-Driven Banking Sector in the UK* [online], Finance Innovation Lab, Available from: https://financeinnovationlab.org/wp-content/uploads/2020/12/Purpose-Driven-Finance-Finance-Innovation-Lab.pdf [Accessed 13 March 2024].

[49] The British Academy (2018) *Reforming Business for the 21st Century: A Framework for the Future of the Corporation* [online], p 9, Available from: www.thebritishacademy.ac.uk/documents/76/Reforming-Business-for-21st-Century-British-Academy.pdf [Accessed 11 March 2024].

embedded in their internal rules on purpose, power and profit (see Chapter Five). A reframed procurement policy to nurture sustainable corporate ownership would amalgamate these two sets of ambitions, reflecting an economic model where state and market partner up to generate, and prioritize, social value, recognizing 'that organizational models themselves have value beyond the core services or products that they provide'.[50] Some would refer to such a model as a 'mission economy' marked by purposeful economic actors and a closer alignment between public and private values.[51] It would not take away resources from VCSE organizations and other SMEs, but expand the agenda to incorporate them. This policy would, via outsourcing contracts, be intended to make financing available to help different types of firms in sustainable ownership grow and expand, compensating for the challenges in accessing capital that they may otherwise face. It would also help plug important other gaps in the support they need to become stronger actors in the current economy. Importantly, it would also create more familiarity with sustainable corporate ownership forms and also help with the development of tailored governance tools, including for the measurement and reporting of their impact.[52]

---

[50] Social Enterprise UK (2023) *Social Value Roadmap 2032* [online], June, p 23, Available from: www.socialenterprise.org.uk/seuk-report/the-soc ial-value-roadmap/ [Accessed 11 March 2024].

[51] Mazzucato, M. (2021) *Mission Economy: A Moonshot Guide to Changing Capitalism*, London: Allen Lane. See also Collington, R. and Mazzucato, M. (2022) *Beyond Outsourcing: Re-Embedding the State in Public Value Production*, UCL Institute for Innovation and Public Purpose Working Paper 2022-14, Available from: www.ucl.ac.uk/bartlett/pub lic-purpose/wp2022-14 [Accessed 27 February 2024].

[52] This could be linked, for example, to the development of standards for measuring social value. See Social Enterprise UK (2023) *Social Value Roadmap 2032* [online], June, p 15, Available from: www.socia lenterprise.org.uk/seuk-report/the-social-value-roadmap/ [Accessed 11 March 2024].

SEVEN

The Legal Framework

Policy design

The incorporation of sustainable corporate ownership into public procurement would require careful planning. The state would have to provide contracting authorities with a clear understanding of its expectations under a new policy, noting especially what is, and is not, expected and possible for contracting authorities to do under the current public procurement legal framework. This policy would also have to be reflected in adjustments to various contracting guidance documents, including the national procurement policy statement,[1] to support these strategic changes. We can expect some of these changes to be relatively uncomplicated. They would effectively refocus the regime on criteria that reflect governance in sustainable corporate ownership, enabling and encouraging contracting authorities to include these criteria in their public procurement as part of their tender evaluation procedure and/or as a condition to tender (reserved procedure), as long as to do so can be considered to align with the overarching delivery of value for money. In doing so, the state would give contracting authorities the option to

---

[1] HM Government (2021) *National Procurement Policy Statement* [online], June, Available from: https://assets.publishing.service.gov.uk/governm ent/uploads/system/uploads/attachment_data/file/990289/National_ Procurement_Policy_Statement.pdf [Accessed 23 February 2024].

specify that private firms contracted to deliver public services demonstrate corporate governance reflecting elements of sustainable ownership and, under certain circumstances, give preference to those that do. In practice, it would be necessary to ask suppliers, when they submit a tender or pre-tender questionnaire, to include their constitutional documentation (in the case of a company, their articles of association) and any other relevant company documentation (for example, shareholder agreements) as evidence of any elements of sustainable ownership design which are incorporated there, including in relation to criteria of corporate purpose (beneficiary rights), decision-making power (control rights) and profit distribution (economic rights).

We can assume that aspects of this transitioning process are relatively low-cost. The state would change its tendering strategy, and while this might require some policy or even legal changes, further demands on resources would be limited, broadly speaking, to providing education and information regarding the new regime. Once a commitment to a new policy has been made, it would be relatively easy to implement in practice initially. The greater challenge would be to ensure the benefits of such a policy are fully realized in the medium term and long term. To assure this, other aspects, including those related to oversight of a new regime, might be more resource intensive and require careful consideration of short- and long-term objectives and an assessment against a number of risks, including its potential impacts on competition and capabilities in service delivery and on existing procurement policies that support VCSE (further discussed later in this chapter).

As well as revising aspects of its current contracting guidance and policy documentation, the government might review certain aspects in the new public procurement legal regime. However, given the very recent introduction of new UK public procurement legislation, we can assume that appetite for immediate further legislative changes will be limited. Were the government to expand its focus on sustainable corporate ownership, this new focus would likely be on how a new policy would be accommodated within this recently introduced UK procurement legal framework, rather than opening discussions on further legal change. Even a new government following the general election in July 2024 would, initially, likely look for continuity and rely on flexibilities within the current law to accommodate sustainable corporate ownership rather than pushing quickly for further reform that might increase these flexibilities. Our discussion should therefore assume that legal rules will likely remain unchanged for a while, but changes to guidance and the national procurement policy statement may happen rather more quickly and unproblematically. With time, however, scope for legal reform may well be considered. Labour in opposition has certainly stressed potential further changes it wishes to see, with its own 'five-point plan' for public procurement including a pledge to produce guidelines to ensure 'contracts are awarded in the public interest' and 'to reward businesses that create local jobs, skills and wealth, treat their workers fairly and pay taxes responsibly, making social value mandatory in all contracts'.[2]

The design of a new policy would be crucial. The state would most likely opt for a permissive policy regime that does not impose a substantive obligation on contracting authorities to incorporate sustainable ownership into their public procurement. Rather, a new policy would leave room for discretion. It could be framed, initially at least, as a procedural obligation that contracting authorities should consider or have regard to the public benefit of sustainable ownership in their public procurement, and this may be expressly incorporated into the government's national procurement policy statement.

---

[2] Procurement with Purpose (2022) 'Labour has a five-point plan for public procurement' [online], 26 September, Available from: www.procurement withpurpose.com/blog/labour-has-a-five-point-plan-for-public-proc urement-social-value-a-core-feature [Accessed 29 February 2024].

According to the new procurement legislation, a contracting authority must have regard to the national procurement policy statement.[3] What this entails would need to be specified, and practice under the Public Services (Social Value) Act 2012 derived from the legal duty in that legislation to 'consider' social value criteria may usefully be taken into account in developing relevant guidance. An alternative, more prescriptive solution would impose a substantive obligation on contracting authorities to evaluate sustainable ownership of potential providers unless doing so would impede their overarching duty to attain value for money. As a considerable shift in policy, the scope of such an obligation would need to be carefully considered and would likely be selectively applied, only in areas where this would be considered necessary – for example, because recent outsourcing problems demonstrate a structural risk.

A policy would need to provide guidance on the criteria that determine sustainable corporate ownership – these would include aspects of purpose, power and profit – but without being overly prescriptive, to enable experimentation. In practice, it would be up to contracting authorities to map bidders against relevant criteria and evaluate their ownership structure. Bidding organizations would be required to submit evidence (typically including their constitutional documentation) in the tendering process, and contracting authorities would be expected to evaluate transparently. To enable an experimental design, contracting authorities should be encouraged to integrate flexibility on how exactly bidding organizations might fulfil the relevant criteria relating to internal rules on purpose, power and profit, rather than being overly prescriptive. The process would, in this sense at least, be rather different from the current testing that happens when, for example, public service

---

[3] Section 13(9) PA2023.

mutuals apply for contracts reserved under the light touch regime, where the legislator has prescriptively set a particular form of sustainable ownership and tests criteria accordingly in a reserved contracts procedure. Again, where a more prescriptive approach would be seen as preferable under an extended policy on sustainable ownership, this would likely be limited to specific sectors.

Flexibility is central, as public procurement can in this way be rebalanced in favour of those that are willing to align themselves with sustainable corporate ownership, creating, in effect, a ratchet effect towards sustainable ownership forms among those willing to tender for public contracts. Such an experimental set-up, including openness as to the design of sustainable ownership in individual provider organizations, has the important effect of allowing contracting authorities to collect information and to build up expertise on the availability and suitability of different sustainable corporate ownership designs to deliver different public contracts. This will be particularly significant in determining the scale and scope of this policy in the long term. Different sustainable ownership forms are likely to suit some contracts better than others: for example, a localized person-centred service might be well served by an organization with profit distribution constraints or a mutual organization, while a looser purpose-driven corporate organization, possibly certified as a B Corp, could be well suited to other complex services, including in the utilities sector.

It can be anticipated that a new policy would take effect gradually as contracting authorities enter into new contracts, rather than imposing an obligation to change existing public services contracts. As with insourcing, it would otherwise potentially be necessary to compensate the shareholders of an existing supplier company that would be required to adopt an alternative sustainable format in order to retain the ability to deliver a public service. Again, as with insourcing, the state can avoid both questions of compensation and potentially costly litigation by limiting the application of a new policy to those windows of opportunity where an existing outsourcing contract expires, meaning a slower gradual rollout.

It would be necessary for government to address and assuage any concern that a reframed policy would undermine the existing efforts to support access for VCSE organizations to public procurement (see Chapters Four and Five). VCSE organizations, operating in the social economy, typically feature elements of sustainable corporate ownership. By expanding a policy towards other forms of sustainable corporate design, including some that would not align with the government's current understanding of VCSE organizations, the intention should not be (nor, more importantly, must the effect be) to withdraw support from VCSE organizations in ways that might undermine their thriving and growth. A new policy would need to realistically assess, and address, the possibility of a potential drift of focus away from the social economy. For example, public contracts that may currently be reserved for VCSE organizations might be handed to purpose-driven but profit-distributing corporate organizations. This extension would be appropriate in some cases – for example, to accommodate contract size and service needs. But in other cases, there may be concerns, perhaps simply because contracting authorities lack awareness of the exact differences between different formats, or because they might be 'a little loose' in evaluating sustainable corporate formats.[4]

These are risks that a well-designed monitoring system and awareness-raising programme could address. Adequately designed, a new policy could in fact strengthen the position of

---

[4]   Taken from a reference to employee ownership and good example of how the government misrepresented a supposedly 'employee-owned' provider that was in fact investor owned – UNISON (2013) *Mutual Benefit? Should Mutuals, Co-Operatives and Social Enterprises Deliver Public Services?* [online], p 23, Available from: www.unison.org.uk/content/uploads/2013/06/On-line-Catalogue199463.pdf [Accessed 27 February 2024].

VCSE organizations by requiring organizations tendering for certain public contracts to map themselves against governance criteria that reflect elements of sustainable corporate ownership. At the same time, it might address risks that contracting authorities will apply existing policies to support procurement from VCSE overly narrowly. Cooperatives UK, for example, raises the following concern:

> Where the [procurement] model is based on broad categories such as VCSE, there is a particular risk that many co-operatives that deliver significant social value will be unreasonably disadvantaged. This is because categories in common usage today, such as for-profit and VCSE do not always accommodate co-operatives. We are especially concerned that worker owned businesses that are well placed to deliver significant social value in government supply chains are usually excluded from VCSE categorisation.[5]

The mapping exercise, which a revised policy would encourage, would reveal what governance qualities each organization brings to the public contract, enabling contracting authorities, more quickly over time, to assess and manage the risk of exploitative contracting behaviour and ensure there is transparency. The transparency within this mapping would deliver an important framework that puts an assessment of sustainable corporate ownership design centre stage. These institutional aspects of the new policy are, therefore, what would likely require most additional resource and long-term planning to ensure that the system

---

[5] Cooperatives UK (2019), 'Consultation response: Social Value in Government Procurement, June, p 5, Available from: https://www. uk.coop/sites/default/files/2020-11/Social%20%20value%20in%20gov ernment%20procurement%20-%20Co-operatives%20UK%20response. pdf [Accessed 26 April 2024].

is adequately institutionalized. One option would be to integrate a procurement policy on sustainable corporate ownership into an expanded social value framework (further discussed later in this chapter).

In implementing a policy on sustainable corporate ownership, the coordinating role of a monitoring body, such as an 'office for public services' or a 'social value council', would be an additional possibility to ensure accountability.[6] This might help expose specific governance issues, including problems that have troubled the VCSE sector in the past – from excessive salary payments to 'sham' trusts or 'fake' non-profits, or a lack of accountability to funders.[7] Given their variation, individual corporate designs should be the subject of some considerable scrutiny: while some rightly see the potential for sustainable economic organizing

---

[6] Social Enterprise UK (2023) *Social Value Roadmap 2032* [online], June, p 15, Available from: www.socialenterprise.org.uk/seuk-report/the-soc ial-value-roadmap/ [Accessed 11 March 2024].

[7] On inflated salaries in non-profits, see Hansmann, H.B. (1980) 'The role of nonprofit enterprise', *The Yale Law Journal*, 89(5): 835–901, p 844. On fake non-profits used as a front by for-profit companies to deliver public services, see Mayo, E. 'Fake non-profits – lies, damned lies and Carillion's non-profit companies', *Ed Mayo's Blog: The Power of Co-Operation* [online], 1 April, Available from: https://edmayo.wordpress.com/2018/02/01/ fake-non-profits-lies-damned-lies-and-carillions-non-profit-compan ies/ [Accessed 28 February 2024]. On "sham" trusts see Cooperatives UK (2019), 'Consultation response: Social Value in Government Procurement, June, p 3, Available from: https://www.uk.coop/sites/ default/files/2020-11/Social%20value%20in%20government%20 procurement%20-%20Co-operatives%20UK%20response.pdf [Accessed 26 April 2024]. In relation to charities hiding behind their social goals to obfuscate accountability to their funders, see House of Commons Public Administration and Constitutional Affairs Committee (2016) *The Collapse of Kids Company: Lessons for Charity Trustees, Professional Firms, the Charity Commission, and Whitehall* [online], 1 February, Available from: https:// publications.parliament.uk/pa/cm201516/cmselect/cmpubadm/433/ 433.pdf [Accessed 28 February 2024].

in these variations of the corporate form, others are legitimately concerned about the possibility of mission drift or 'greenwashing'.[8] A suitable institutional design could also monitor the long-term effects of a new policy, including by assessing the risk of creating new incumbencies and dependencies, and the extent to which sustainably owned firms that deliver public services manage to penetrate private markets. An oversight body would be able to address how nurturing providers in sustainable ownership to achieve independence can be successful. On current data, most public service mutuals appear to continue their dependency on a single or small number of public contracts for several years.[9] Other evidence suggests that social procurement initiatives rarely generate effects beyond procurement markets.[10] More data over time would be helpful to give a fuller picture.

8   Ebrahim, A., Battilana, J. and Mair, J. (2014) 'The governance of social enterprises: mission drift and accountability challenges in hybrid organizations', *Research in Organizational Behavior*, 34: 81–100. Armour, J., Enriques, L. and Wetzer, T. (2022) *Green Pills: Making Corporate Climate Commitments Credible*, European Corporate Governance Institute Working Paper No 657/2022 [online], 1 December, Available from: http://dx.doi.org/10.2139/ssrn.4190268 [Accessed 27 February 2024].

9   Vickers, I., Lyon, F., Sepulveda, L. and Brennan, G. (2021) *Public Service Mutuals: Transforming How Services Are Delivered through Social Enterprise and Democratic Governance?* [online], Centre for Enterprise and Economic Development Research and Middlesex University, in cooperation with Social Enterprise UK, January, pp 12–15, Available from: https:// assets.publishing.service.gov.uk/media/630f64978fa8f544842c49b3/ Public_Service_Mutuals_Longitudinal_Case_Study.pdf [Accessed 27 February 2024].

10   Strupler Leiser, M. and Wolter, S.C. (2017) 'Empirical evidence on the effectiveness of social public procurement policy: the case of the Swiss apprenticeship training system', *Labour: Review of Labour Economics and Industrial Relations*, 31(2): 204–222.

Reserved contracts

With limited exceptions,[11] UK contracting authorities are not expected to award public contracts directly to an individual supplier without having engaged in some form of competitive procedure.[12] However, modifications to competition are accepted, and indeed anticipated, for contracts that are smaller and therefore fall below the regulated procurement thresholds.[13] Similarly, for those contracts which relate to certain mainly person-centred services, including health, social care and education, adjustments to competitive procurement principles can be made under a more light touch regulatory regime.[14] Here, contracts may under certain conditions be reserved for organizations operating as public service mutuals (discussed in Chapter Five).[15] The main justifications for these modifications, especially in the case of smaller contracts

---

[11] See the direct awards procedures in the Health Care Services (Provider Selection Regime) Regulations 2023. In addition, the PA2023 allows for specific limited circumstances that justify a direct award – see sections 40–43 and Schedule 5 PA2023. These include 'user choice contracts', mainly to provide for individualized care.

[12] The government has clarified that even for contracts below the regulated procurement threshold, 'value for money will not be achieved by direct award' – Cabinet Office (2021) *A Guide to Reserving Below Threshold Procurements* [online], p 3, Available from: https://assets.publishing.serv ice.gov.uk/government/uploads/system/uploads/attachment_data/file/ 1014494/20210818-A-Guide-to-Reserving-Below-Threshold-Procu rements.pdf [Accessed 27 February 2024].

[13] Public Procurement (Agreement on Government Procurement) (Thresholds) (Amendment) Regulations 2023.

[14] See Schedule 1 of the draft Procurement Act 2023 (Miscellaneous Provisions) Regulations 2024, Available from: https://assets.publish ing.service.gov.uk/government/uploads/system/uploads/attachme nt_data/file/1163167/230615_DRAFT_Procurement_Act_2023__ Miscellaneous_Provisions__Regulations_2024_-_consultation_version. pdf [Accessed 29 February 2024].

[15] See section 33 PA2023, and the analogous regime for supported employment providers in section 32 PA2023.

and including the possibility of reserving contracts for some types of supplier, relate primarily to certain idiosyncratic or non-contractible aspects of the services in question that mean local providers, SMEs or VCSE organizations may typically be better placed to deliver value for money on these contracts than others, taking into account primary (price and quality) and secondary (social value) considerations.[16] This, however, still depends on the existence of a thriving community of smaller, social or local suppliers that can meet such demand.[17] Contracting authorities are still expected to consider whether a reserved procedure secures value for money.[18] They will be

[16] Cabinet Office (2020) *Procurement Policy Note – Reserving Below Threshold Procurements*, Action Note PPN 11/20 [online], December, Available from: https://assets.publishing.service.gov.uk/media/614c9c0fe90e077a2 e2adc44/20210923-PPN-11_20-Reserving-Below-Threshold-Procu rements.docx.pdf [Accessed 26 February 2024].

[17] Department for Digital, Culture, Media, and Sport (2022) *The Role of Voluntary, Community, and Social Enterprise (VCSE) Organisations in Public Procurement* [online], August, Available from: https://assets.publishing.serv ice.gov.uk/government/uploads/system/uploads/attachment_data/file/ 1100749/The_role_of_Voluntary__Community__and_Social_Enterp rises_in_public_procurement.pdf [Accessed 27 February 2024].

[18] Cabinet Office (2021) *A Guide to Reserving Below Threshold Procurements* [online], pp 2–3, Available from: https://assets.publishing.service.gov. uk/government/uploads/system/uploads/attachment_data/file/1014 494/20210818-A-Guide-to-Reserving-Below-Threshold-Procureme nts.pdf [Accessed 27 February 2024]. Cabinet Office (2020) *Procurement Policy Note – Reserving Below Threshold Procurements*, Action Note PPN 11/20 [online], December, p 4, Available from: https://assets. publishing.service.gov.uk/media/614c9c0fe90e077a2e2adc44/20210 923-PPN-11_20-Reserving-Below-Threshold-Procurements.docx. pdf [Accessed 26 February 2024]. HM Treasury (2022) *The Green Book: Central Government Guidance on Appraisal and Evaluation* [online], June, p 52, Available from: www.gov.uk/government/publications/the- green-book-appraisal-and-evaluation-in-central-governent [Accessed 26 February 2024]. HM Treasury (2023) *Managing Public Money* [online], May, Available from: https://assets.publishing.service.gov.uk/media/ 65c4a3773f634b001242c6b7/Managing_Public_Money_-_May_202 3_2.pdf [Accessed 26 February 2024].

expected to carry out due diligence, verifying the supplier meets the relevant criteria by asking questions, but without a full pre-qualification stage, which would likely be considered disproportionate.[19]

A policy to support sustainable corporate ownership could be integrated into this existing regime relatively easily. The government would simply change or supplement its current contracting guidance relating to the reservation of below-threshold contracts to integrate wording to accommodate criteria for sustainable corporate ownership. For example, a generic pre-tender question applicable to below-threshold contracts might read as follows:

To be eligible to participate in this tender, please demonstrate that your organization operates in sustainable corporate ownership. To demonstrate this, please provide information that may relate to:

(a) the legal status of your organization;
(b) the legally defined purpose of your organization;
(c) rules and procedures relating to your organization's governance and control; and
(d) rules and procedures relating the retaining, transfer or distribution of profits or assets by your organization.

Please provide any relevant information, including evidence, by supplying a copy (or link) to the constitutional or founding documents of your organization and any other documentation that you consider relevant.

---

[19] Cabinet Office (2021) *A Guide to Reserving Below Threshold Procurements* [online], p 5, Available from: https://assets.publishing.service.gov.uk/government/uploads/system/uploads/attachment_data/file/1014494/20210818-A-Guide-to-Reserving-Below-Threshold-Procurements.pdf [Accessed 27 February 2024].

In a more far-reaching move, which would involve changes to the agreed procurement legal framework, to provide for greater flexibility the government might consider an extension of the set-aside for reservable light touch services, making it available to suppliers in sustainable corporate ownership beyond public service mutuals. The regime could potentially be opened up to a spectrum of suppliers, provided that these legal changes could be agreed. Hypothetically, legislation might extend the ability to reserve contracts even further, permitting contracting authorities to afford suppliers in sustainable corporate ownership preferential treatment for a wider range of public contracts, including potentially for less localized or person-centred services. A rationale that might support sustainably owned suppliers may, for example, apply to other complex public contracts with non-contractible elements, such as those for the delivery of important consultancy services or a software system to organize vital aspects of key public services, such as healthcare, postal services, prison management, immigration centres or railways (some of which will of course be large contracts).

But a reserved procedure of this scope would be controversial (see also the discussion and literature in Chapter One). The substantive concern is that preferential treatment of any type of provider narrows competition, missing efficiencies and leaving other private capacities potentially untapped, to the detriment of the state as public consumer and of the citizens it provides for. The implementation of such an extended opportunity to reserve contracts for sustainable corporate ownership would, therefore, have to be assessed carefully against the impact on competition in public procurement and capabilities in service delivery. The state may not be able to attain value for money, or even to tender at all, where there are simply not enough suitable providers – especially given the scope of some projects and need for their capitalization – ready to tender for public contracts by mapping themselves against the criteria of sustainable corporate ownership. We can expect this to create difficulties given the current predominance of commercial providers, not least as strategic suppliers.[20] The state may accept some competitive constraints and their negative cost implications only if in the medium or long term it considers this to be an effective strategy not just to significantly reduce failings in public service outsourcing and improve outcomes, but also to address wider problems of exploitation that are closely linked to the dominance of overly extractive forms of corporate ownership in the wider economy. Reducing constraints on supply-side competition among sustainably owned suppliers would require time, resources and determination. On the other hand, provided that a new procurement policy would be sufficiently resourced and well designed and instrumentalized, these are not intransigent problems – they can be solved over time. And there is no reason to believe, a priori, that nurturing sustainable corporate ownership will be more resource-intensive than other governance solutions to outsourcing failures, all of which have their challenges too (see Chapters Three and Four). The more substantial challenge, arguably, lies in overcoming inertia and political opposition to challenging the status quo.

Finally, a new policy would have to consider separately how to address healthcare services that are regulated under the new and separate provider selection regime from 2023.[21] Under this new selection regime, there is currently no option to reserve contracting opportunities, even for smaller contracts. Sustainably owned corporate providers may of course be selected in any of the direct award procedures under this regime if relevant conditions are satisfied, or in a more flexible 'most suitable provider' process that does not require a full tender. But

---

[20] In relation to the non-profit sector, it has been recognized that '[b]ecause there are rarely a large number of non-profit organizations in a given human services market, normal market forces cannot ensure efficiency' – Brown, L.K. and Troutt, E. (2004) 'Funding relations between nonprofits and government: a positive example', *Nonprofit and Voluntary Sector Quarterly*, 33(1): 5–27, p 9.

[21] Health Care Services (Provider Selection Regime) Regulations 2023.

these procedures do not currently make specific provision for any particular form of provider. Instead, relevant contracting authorities are expected to treat VCSE, commercial, NHS or public providers on a level playing field.[22]

Quality

Under the new public procurement legislation, contracting authorities are expected to evaluate suppliers and award the contract to the supplier that submits the 'most advantageous tender'.[23] Unlike under the previous EU-based procurement regime, no reference is made in the new law to price or cost. Hypothetically, then, provided their public budgets permit it, a contracting authority may select suppliers exclusively on the basis of quality-related award criteria, including criteria related to delivering social value providing wider social, economic and environmental well-being (see Chapter One). In practice, however, we can expect that budgetary constraints will continue to mean contracting authorities' focus is on cost and price. In any event, they are expected to have regard to delivering value for money as well as maximizing public benefit in their procurement.[24] For those healthcare services which are now regulated under the new provider selection regime, key criteria are more fully set out in the regulation as relating to quality and innovation; value; integration, collaboration

---

[22] See NHS England (2023) 'The Provider Selection Regime: statutory guidance' [online], updated 21 February 2024, Available from: www.engl and.nhs.uk/long-read/the-provider-selection-regime-statutory-guida nce/ [Accessed 29 February 2024].

[23] Section 19(2) PA2023.

[24] Section 12(1) PA2023. See the House of Lords parliamentary debate on 13 July 2022, in particular: Procurement Bill [HL], volume 823, debated on Wednesday 13 July 2022, Baroness Worthington, column 517GC, Available from: https://hansard.parliament.uk/Lords/2022-07-13/debates/E4A9A7A3-E3DD-433F-BFE8-FCEA6FE4822B/ProcurementBill(HL) [Accessed 14 April 2024].

and service sustainability; improving access, reducing health inequalities and facilitating choice; social value.[25]

Under the procurement legislation, award criteria are expected to be sufficiently clear, measurable, specific and proportionate.[26] In particular, under the general procurement regime, they must relate to the subject matter of the contract.[27] This provides continuity with the previous EU-based regime's requirement that criteria be 'linked to the subject-matter of the public contract in question'.[28] Although its practical benefits have never been particularly well documented, this requirement has now seemingly been further endorsed by the UK legislator.[29] In order for contracting authorities to consider sustainable corporate ownership in their evaluation of different bids, therefore, it must

---

[25] Section 5 Health Care Services (Provider Selection Regime) Regulations 2023.

[26] Note, the focus here is on award criteria and not on conditions of participation (formerly selection criteria). Sustainable corporate ownership would not be considered a 'condition of participation' under the new legislation, as these only include aspects that relate to the bidder's legal and financial capacity, or technical ability, to perform the contract. See section 22(1) PA2023.

[27] Section 23(2) PA2023. In relation to the draft provider selection regime, note in section 5 the absence of a requirement that key criteria must relate to the subject matter of the contract. Nor is this specified in the statutory guidance – NHS England (2023) 'The Provider Selection Regime: statutory guidance' [online], updated 21 February 2024, Available from: www.england.nhs.uk/long-read/the-provider-select ion-regime-statutory-guidance/ [Accessed 29 February 2024].

[28] Section 67(2) Public Contracts Regulations 2015.

[29] For critical discussion of the 'link to the subject matter' criterion under EU public procurement law, see Semple, A. (2015) 'The link to the subject-matter: a glass ceiling for sustainable public contracts?', in B. Sjåfjell and A. Wiesbrock (eds) Sustainable Public Procurement under EU Law. New Perspectives on the State as Stakeholder, Cambridge: Cambridge University Press, pp 50–74. Sanchez-Graells, A. (2019) 'Public procurement and "core" human rights: a sketch of the EU legal framework', in O. Martin-Ortega and C.M. O'Brien (eds) Public Procurement and Human Rights: Risks, Dilemmas and Opportunities for the State as a Buyer, Cheltenham: Edward Elgar, pp 96–114.

be formulated as a criterion that relates to the subject matter of the contract, is clear and measurable, and is proportionate having regard to the nature, complexity and cost of the contract.

One option is to formulate specific quality criteria that suppliers in sustainable corporate ownership might, because of the way their corporate design impacts on their governance, find easier to satisfy and score higher on than others. An award criterion that focuses on workforce satisfaction or engagement might have this effect. We have seen that employee ownership, for example, can improve employee engagement, offering some 'instrumental' benefits: by improving staff motivation, satisfaction and productivity, it improves service delivery.[30] We may extend this also to wider stakeholder engagement and the co-production of service design. The government's bid evaluation guidance, in fact, expressly acknowledges that 'supplier culture and values' can be important in evaluating qualitative aspects of the bid to ensure their instrumental advantages for delivering services:

> Where it is relevant and proportionate it may be possible to evaluate how culture is demonstrated through the bidder's proposals. For example, in a service reliant on a significant number of public facing staff, it may be possible to look at how the bidder proposes to ensure that staff are motivated, happy and content in their work (which can impact on how the service is delivered).[31]

---

[30] Mutuals Taskforce (2012) 'Mutual and cooperative approaches to delivering local services', written evidence before the House of Commons Communities and Local Government Committee [online], May, Available from: https://publications.parliament.uk/pa/cm201213/cmselect/cmcomloc/112/112we08.htm [Accessed 27 February 2024].

[31] HM Government Commercial Function (2021) *Bid Evaluation: Guidance Note* [online], May, p 17, Available from: https://assets.publishing.serv ice.gov.uk/government/uploads/system/uploads/attachment_data/file/987130/Bid_evaluation_guidance_note_May_2021.pdf [Accessed 29 February 2024].

The new legislation, too, suggests some flexibility for contracting authorities in this regard. In order to link a criterion to the subject matter of the contract, they may reference, for example, 'management or organisation of staff where those factors are likely to make a material difference to the quality of goods, services and works supplied'.[32] The contracting authority may, therefore, consider a criterion asking suppliers to demonstrate what processes they will put in place to ensure employees are engaged in delivering the services in question. Such a criterion would be quite specific, and it would address sustainable corporate ownership design in the tendering process, but indirectly: the point is that such processes may be easier for sustainably owned providers – which, by design, engage employees as members and decision makers – to demonstrate.

An alternative approach would address corporate ownership design more directly, but this would typically mean framing a relevant tender criterion more openly while still ensuring it relates to the subject matter of the contract. We may even consider the following rather open-ended formulation:

> *How does the corporate ownership of your organization impact on the quality of the services that you will deliver under the contract? In demonstrating ownership, you may refer to:*
>
> *(a) the legal status of your organization;*
> *(b) the legally defined purpose of your organization;*
> *(c) relevant rules and procedures relating to your organization's governance and control; and*
> *(d) relevant rules and procedures relating to the retaining, transfer or distribution of profits or assets by your organization.*

To encourage the use of more ownership-directed tender questions, the government would need to provide some

---

[32] Section 23(5) PA2023.

reassurance for contracting authorities of their compatibility with the relevant legal provisions and set out some guidance by adjusting bid evaluation guides and model contracts, for example.[33] The relevant guidance may be formulated in terms of risk management, which for all public sector organizations is considered 'an essential and integral part of planning and decision-making'.[34] In public procurement this encompasses commercial risks, including, according to the Cabinet Office, risk of 'poor performance by suppliers' or a failure 'to meet all or part of their obligations', which may include exploitation of their contracting obligations.[35] Therefore, the contracting authority would, in the tender documentation, be asking for evidence of how the provider organization proposes to address these risks, while highlighting that sustainable corporate ownership can in fact provide such evidence that commercial risks will be mitigated. The proportionality threshold would

---

[33] The EU procurement legislation which applied in the UK before the new law came into force clarified in its preamble that 'the condition of a link with the subject-matter of the contract excludes criteria and conditions relating to general corporate policy, which cannot be considered as a factor characterising the specific process of production or provision of the purchased works, supplies or services. Contracting authorities should hence not be allowed to require tenderers to have a certain corporate social or environmental responsibility policy in place' – EU Directive 20014/24, Preamble, Article 97. The new UK legislation, the PA2023, contains no such wording but addressing corporate ownership may give rise to similar concerns for the procurement teams in contracting authorities that would have to draft the relevant award criteria.

[34] UK Government (2023) *The Orange Book: Management of Risk – Principles and Concepts* [online], p 3, Available from: https://assets.publishing.service.gov.uk/government/uploads/system/uploads/attachment_data/file/1154709/HMT_Orange_Book_May_2023.pdf [Accessed 29 February 2024].

[35] Cabinet Office (2021) *A Guide to Reserving Below Threshold Procurements* [online], p 3, Available from: https://assets.publishing.service.gov.uk/government/uploads/system/uploads/attachment_data/file/1014494/20210818-A-Guide-to-Reserving-Below-Threshold-Procurements.pdf [Accessed 27 February 2024].

be satisfied particularly where complex and person-centred contracts are being tendered, including a higher proportion of non-contractible elements. It should be clear that where contracting authorities include evidence of sustainable ownership design as part of their award criteria (unlike for a reserved contract), this would invite bidders to map themselves against these characteristics but would not, in principle, prevent commercial bidders from putting in bids. It would simply mean that they will receive no or few points in relation to these criteria, thus disadvantaging them in that respect compared to those bidders that score better on the criteria.

Contracting authorities will need to relate this evidence clearly to the subject matter of the contract. In that respect, the legislation makes clear that wider commercial assessments can play their role: in order to link a criterion to the subject matter of the contract, contracting authorities may reference any 'other costs or value for money in all the circumstances'.[36] This could also include any anticipated mitigation costs that may arise where risks of contractual exploitation are significant. Corporate ownership is, of course, by design a characteristic that relates to the organization generally, not a particular contract – firms (seen here as one legal corporate entity rather than, say, a parent and subsidiary) cannot be 'owned' in one way for one activity and differently for another. But as has been discussed throughout this book, corporate ownership can also be an instrument to ensure that corporate governance processes in the organization align more closely with public governance so that risks that the supplier might exploit incomplete contractual obligations are reduced. Instead, as a direct consequence of the governance incentives derived from sustainable ownership, suppliers are more likely to fill gaps and uncertainties in incomplete contracts in ways that the public authority would have done had they anticipated the gaps and uncertainties in the first place. To put this a different

---

[36] Section 23(5) PA2023.

way, how a contract is delivered (quality) and who delivers it (key elements of ownership) are so closely linked in the case of complex contracts that even though ownership design inevitably applies to the organization, not just to the contract, both are complementary aspects of the qualitative evaluation criterion that relates to the delivery of the service in question. Both, therefore, relate to the subject matter of the contract.

Social value

The use of social value criteria in evaluating suppliers has grown among contracting authorities over the past decade, following the enactment of the Public Services (Social Value) Act 2012. With these criteria, they evaluate the impact of a public contract on the wider social, economic and environmental well-being in the relevant area (see further Chapter One). The Act itself is relatively limited in scope, requiring contracting authorities to consider (not actually evaluate) social value criteria only when they procure large public service contracts.[37] However, local authorities have made some progress in applying social value more widely, and central government recently developed these obligations further by introducing an obligation in all central government procurement for social value to be evaluated, accounting for at least 10 per cent of the total score in the tender evaluation.[38] It remains a requirement that social value criteria must be clear, precise and proportionate, and related

---

[37] Section 1(3) Public Services (Social Value) Act 2012.

[38] HM Government (2020) *Procurement Policy Note – Taking Account of Social Value in the Award of Central Government Contracts*, Action Note PPN 06/20 [online], September, pt 2 and 12, Available from: https:// assets.publishing.service.gov.uk/government/uploads/system/uploads/ attachment_data/file/921437/PPN-06_20-Taking-Account-of-Social-Value-in-the-Award-of-Central-Government-Contracts.pdf [Accessed 26 February 2024]. For social value guidance in NHS procurement, see NHS (2022) 'Applying net zero and social value in the procurement

to the subject matter of the contract. Social value is also now listed as a national priority outcome for the public benefit in the current national procurement policy statement, to which contracting authorities must have regard under the new procurement legislation for the majority of procurements.[39] It is expressly listed as a key criterion under the new provider selection regime for certain healthcare services.[40] It is not, however, included directly in the general public procurement legislation. The government meanwhile has developed detailed guidance and a 'social value model' which central government authorities are expected to follow in applying social value criteria. The model itself was developed drawing on examples of best practice in applying social value in local government.[41]

of NHS goods and services' [online], 1 March, Available from: www. england.nhs.uk/greenernhs/wp-content/uploads/sites/51/2022/03/ B1030-applying-net-zero-and-social-value-nhs-goods-and-services.pdf [Accessed 29 February 2024].

[39] Section 13(9) PA2023. Cabinet Office (2021) *Procurement Policy Note – National Procurement Policy Statement*, Action Note PPN 05/21 [online], June, pt 10, Available from: https://assets.publishing.service.gov.uk/ media/60b0c01d8fa8f5488e618b93/PPN_05_21-_National_Procu rement_Policy_Statement.pdf [Accessed 26 February 2024]. See also HM Government (2021) *National Procurement Policy Statement* [online], June, Available from: https://assets.publishing.service.gov.uk/governm ent/uploads/system/uploads/attachment_data/file/990289/National_ Procurement_Policy_Statement.pdf [Accessed 23 February 2024].

[40] Section 5 Health Care Services (Provider Selection Regime) Regulations 2023.

[41] Cabinet Office and Department for Culture, Media and Sport (2020) *Procurement Policy Note – Taking Account of Social Value in the Award of Central Government Contracts*, Action Note PPN 06/20 [online], September, pt 8, Available from: https://assets.publishing.service.gov. uk/government/uploads/system/uploads/attachment_data/file/921437/ PPN-06_20-Taking-Account-of-Social-Value-in-the-Award-of-Central- Government-Contracts.pdf [Accessed 26 February 2024]. Government Commercial Function (2020) *The Social Value Model* [online], December, Available from: https://assets.publishing.service.gov.uk/media/5fc8b 7ede90e0762a0d71365/Social-Value-Model-Edn-1.1-3-Dec-20.pdf

The individual themes for which social value criteria are formulated as part of the model are relatively far-reaching and specific: COVID-19 recovery; economic inequality; climate change; equal opportunity; and well-being.[42] So too are the social value outcomes (each with relevant sub-criteria) developed as part of the current national procurement policy statement, to which authorities must have regard: creating new businesses, new jobs and new skills; tackling climate change and reducing waste; and improving supplier diversity, innovation and resilience.[43] There is, across these documents, considerable detail in the guidance on formulating effective social value criteria.

The application of these social value criteria can support suppliers in sustainable corporate ownership indirectly because they may be well set up, as a result of their ownership and internal governance model, to deliver services that support wider economic, social and environmental well-being. The

---

[Accessed 26 February 2024]. Government Commercial Function (2020) *Guide to Using the Social Value Model* [online], December, Available from: https://assets.publishing.service.gov.uk/media/5fc8b804d3bf7 f7f53e5a503/Guide-to-using-the-Social-Value-Model-Edn-1.1-3-Dec-20.pdf [Accessed 26 February 2024]. HM Government (2023) *The Sourcing Playbook* [online], June, p 62, Available from: https://assets.pub lishing.service.gov.uk/media/64901fcc5f7bb700127fac5e/Sourcing_Pla ybook_Final.pdf [Accessed 26 February 2024].

[42] Cabinet Office and Department for Culture, Media and Sport (2020) *Procurement Policy Note – Taking Account of Social Value in the Award of Central Government Contracts*, Action Note PPN 06/20 [online], September, Annex A, Available from: https://assets.publishing.service. gov.uk/government/uploads/system/uploads/attachment_data/file/921 437/PPN-06_20-Taking-Account-of-Social-Value-in-the-Award-of-Central-Government-Contracts.pdf [Accessed 26 February 2024].

[43] HM Government (2021) *National Procurement Policy Statement* [online], June, pt 13, Available from: https://assets.publishing.service.gov. uk/government/uploads/system/uploads/attachment_data/file/ 990289/National_Procurement_Policy_Statement.pdf [Accessed 23 February 2024].

more weight contracting authorities accredit to social value criteria, the less they will focus narrowly on price. The following passage from Cooperatives UK, worth quoting in full, illustrates these opportunities:

> Different types of provider – not only SMEs and VCSEs but also worker-owned businesses and mission-led businesses – have corporate purposes, organisational structures and *modus operandi* which can make them better-placed to deliver on particular social value outcomes. For example, worker-owned businesses are especially effective at providing good work and sharing opportunity, influence and reward broadly among a wide range of people in supply chains. In [one] example, the way 'freelancer co-operatives' can provide a practicable, empowering and rewarding means for smaller businesses and freelancers to participate in government supply chains should certainly not be overlooked. To take one more different example, some types of VCSE provider have organisational and delivery models that empower local communities and end-users, which can significantly enhance the quality of co-production, while nurturing and mobilising social capital to deliver better outcomes.[44]

But in relation to other forms of social value – for example, providing work placements, apprenticeships and training schemes – large commercial providers might in fact have an advantage in their delivery, given their resources and skill set. And there clearly is interest among commercial firms, including

---

[44] Cooperatives UK (2019), 'Consultation response: Social Value in Government Procurement, June, p 2, Available from: https://www. uk.coop/sites/default/files/2020-11/Social%20%20value%20in%20gov ernment%20procurement%20-%20Co-operatives%20UK%20response. pdf [Accessed 26 April 2024]. Footnotes omitted.

large corporations, to develop their capabilities to deliver social value criteria in order to attract public contracts.[45] To support sustainable corporate ownership in its social value model, the state would therefore need to develop clearly a metric that 'links different types of business ownership and control to particular social value outcomes'.[46]

Social value criteria that *directly* address the development of sustainable corporate ownership as a secondary benefit of public procurement could also be further extended. For example, improving supplier diversity, including through support for startups, SMEs and VCSE organizations, has been developed as a social value criterion to help with creating 'diverse supply chains' to deliver public contracts. The government could instead choose to expand the criterion to address enterprise diversity and the development of sustainable corporate ownership designs more fully, including among primary suppliers. The current support for developing new businesses as a social value objective could be refocused in much the same way to support the creation of new forms of sustainable corporate ownership. Both criteria are, under the current social value model, sub-criteria to an overarching theme that addresses 'tackling economic inequality' as part of delivering social value. But in a new policy on sustainable corporate ownership, the government could move to directly address its central cause, namely, the existence of extractive corporate

---

[45] Social Enterprise UK (2023) *Social Value Roadmap 2032* [online], June, Available from: www.socialenterprise.org.uk/seuk-report/the-social-value-roadmap/ [Accessed 11 March 2024]. Social Enterprise UK (2022), *Creating a Social Value Economy* [online], Available from: https://www.socialenterprise.org.uk/app/uploads/2022/05/Social-Value-2032-Creating-a-Social-Value-Economy-compressed.pdf [Accessed 26 April 2024].

[46] Cooperatives UK (2019), 'Consultation response: Social Value in Government Procurement, June, p 3, Available from: https://www.uk.coop/sites/default/files/2020-11/Social%20value%20in%20government%20procurement%20-%20Co-operatives%20UK%20response.pdf [Accessed 26 April 2024]. Footnotes omitted.

design enabling rentier investors to extract value from labour. Nurturing the sort of firm that while profit-making is also less extractive than a company run purely to maximize profits for its shareholders goes to the heart of what delivering social value for society can be about.

Conclusion

As the new UK procurement law comes into operation, addressing public outsourcing problems remains a difficult and gradual process where, despite their versatility, traditional governance tools in contract design, public markets and regulation all have demonstrable imperfections. Reintroducing public ownership, replacing contractual governance with a public governance regime, is an important alternative intervention, but it bears uncertainties as to whether, in the long term, the state can effectively provide ambitious public welfare without entering into extensive strategic partnerships with private actors. Far from shrinking its responsibilities, the state often uses private actors to achieve, through outsourcing, ambitions that demand additional capacity and capabilities. This is a perfect example of the interdependence of and synergies between market and state in delivering a common good.

Trying to identify alternative governance solutions, this book asks whether innovation is possible by expanding an already existing, but currently rather limited and confined, policy to co-opt corporate governance in sustainably owned firms into the contractual governance of public outsourcing instruments in order to reduce (though not fully avoid) the risk of exploitative and extractive behaviour by private partners. An extended policy, expanding the government's current initiatives to support VCSE organizations, would more fully accommodate the flexibilities available in corporate law to design supplementary governance solutions to common problems in public service outsourcing: it would encourage, even expect, contracting authorities to consider, in their outsourcing decisions, the sustainable corporate ownership design of their suppliers, with the aim of improving outsourcing while nurturing more sustainable corporate market actors.

Corporate organizations in sustainable ownership cover a spectrum of governance options, all of which temper financialization and avoid purely extractive design. These organizations are more diverse than those operating as VCSE organizations in the social economy; they include purpose-driven profit-distributing firms, stakeholder-controlled companies, foundation ownership and mutually owned firms. UK company law leaves room for individual companies to reconfigure beneficiary rights, control rights and economic rights in the corporate organization 'away' from the investor-centric default model and towards economic, environmental and social sustainability objectives. To what extent corporate organizations make sensible use of this flexibility is a matter of some complexity, but it seems crucially important for government to assume a role through its public procurement in nurturing this experimentation in sustainable corporate ownership designs, enabling new forms to establish themselves and grow, including in the social and wider economy.

The proposals in this book encourage government to consider taking these initiatives into procurement in more public service sectors, including utilities and infrastructure, where currently to do so is not typical – and outsourcing problems clearly exist. In practice, this change would encourage contracting authorities to *regularly* select providers in sustainable ownership whose corporate governance they consider to be aligned more closely with their own objective to obtain public value, reducing risks of opportunism in the contracting relationship. The approach offers the state an opportunity to potentially harness the advantages of public and private governance *together*. It still brings the benefit of flexibilities that private actors tend to offer and a degree of choice. But it reduces the risk (and cost) that contracts are exploited due to their incompleteness or dependencies, because public and private objectives under this contracting model are more aligned than in the case of public sector contracting with financialized corporate providers. It means reviewing public procurement policy and potentially even adjusting public procurement law further to ensure flexibility for contracting authorities to select sustainably owned suppliers whose design – reflected in the configuration of their internal rules on purpose, power and profit – might render them particularly suited to delivering the public service in question. It would not mean neglecting other forms of control that the state has available – from contractual mechanisms to, in certain cases, re-internalizing public services – but rather supplementing them with an additional focus on public procurement centred on sustainable corporate ownership, aligning with sustainability initiatives in the wider economy.

Index

References to notes show both the page number
and the note number (123n3).